"Jeanne Zornes addresses the most common pitfalls and obstacles that hinder our trust and faith in God. Whether your life is currently traveling on a smooth freeway or a bumpy back-woods trail, you'll gain valuable insight from *When I Got on the Highway to Heaven, I Didn't Expect Rocky Roads!*"

Kathy Collard Miller
Author of *When Counting to Ten Isn't Enough, Staying Friends with Your Kids, When the Honeymoon's Over* and 25 other books.

When I Got on the Highway to Heaven . . .

I Didn't Expect Rocky Roads

Jeanne Zornes

Harold Shaw Publishers
Wheaton, Illinois

ISBN 0-87788-857-4

Edited by Robert Bittner

Cover design by David LaPlaca

Library of Congress Cataloging-in-Publication Data

Zornes, Jeanne, 1947-
    When I got on the highway to heaven, I didn't expect rocky roads! : encouragement for the journey / by Jeanne Zornes ; foreword by Lucinda Secrest McDowell.
        p.   cm.
    Includes bibliographical references.
    1. Christian life. 2. Bible. O.T. Exodus—Criticism, interpretation, etc.
I. Title.
BV4501.2.Z648 1998
248.4—dc21   97-43229
                                                          CIP

03   02   01   00   99   98
10   9   8   7   6   5   4   3   2   1

For Hilton & Lorna Jarvis—
Thanks for being there
when I hit some
of my rocky roads

Contents

Foreword

I first met Jeanne Zornes almost twenty years ago. She had come from the West Coast. I had come from the East Coast. We met in the middle—the Chicago area to be exact. Our common goal was a graduate degree in communication. And though on the surface we seemed quite different, there were some striking similarities.

We were both in our twenties, loved to write, and felt absolutely *certain* (with the bravado only the young can claim) that somehow God was going to use our writing to *spread his love to a hurting world.*

Imagine such presumption! But, even in the 1970s, we had known Jesus long enough to understand that truly he does use clay pots in which to pour out his glory. I'm sure it comes as no surprise to God that today I am writing the foreword to Jeanne's third book, even as she prays for the completion of my own third book. We haven't exactly changed the world, but amazingly enough God has seen fit to use our gifts to encourage others in their faith.

Once again we live on opposite coasts—Jeanne in the mountains of Washington state and I in a lush New England village. Yet we have shared a bond through the years. That "in-between time" from grad school to middle-aged mother-hood has been quite a journey for both of us. No wonder Jeanne calls the highway to heaven a rocky road!

What took place in between our dreams of youth and our current grasp of each day of life God gives is what this book is about: hurting people. Our own hurts. All Christians face challenges and catastrophes and crises and cry out to God, "I can't bear it any longer!" or "I'm afraid!" or "Why me?" Have you ever grumbled or complained in such a way? Then read on and discover great encouragement for your journey.

This book serves as an encouragement in just the ways that communicate best! Jeanne uses biblical examples and the needs each of us faces every day to present modern stories of overcomers—ordinary people (just like you and me) who found God to be Enough on their own rocky roads. Jeanne's style is marvelously personal and humorous, communicating Truth in an easy-to-grasp way. She even provides discussion starters at the end of each chapter for small groups or personal "homework."

I couldn't put down this book. It came at a time when I was about to embark on an international journey outwardly and a spiritual journey inwardly. I not only found strength and inspiration here, but I also felt a deep desire to get to know better all the folk in this book—Dan, Nancy, Lorna, Doug & Shirley, not to mention Moses and God!

Many Christians through the years have written about the life of faith as a journey. I heartily recommend Jeanne's book as a great addition to this collection. The nineteenth-century poet Christina Rossetti summed it up this way,

> Does the road wind up-hill all the way?
> Yes, to the very end.
> Will the day's journey take the whole long day?
> From morn to night, my friend. . . .
> Traveling mercies to you, friend and pilgrim.

Lucinda Secrest McDowell
"Gracehaven"
Wethersfield, CT

Acknowledgments

Writers are often asked where they get their ideas. For me, the place where ideas are born is like the 5 P.M. panic hour in the kitchen. I have pots bubbling, the oven crackling, the microwave purring, cold things jelling, and children so hungry they're digging into the forbidden cache of chocolate chip cookies in the freezer. Somehow I produce a dinner that my family celebrates for a whole ten minutes.

This book represents a lot of ideas simmering on back burners, plus a few things that seemed to pop out of the toaster at just the right time. Trust me, it took more than an hour of panic to pull together! This book started "cooking" during a Bible study of Moses' life. I found the study fascinating and convicting. A pastor turned up the heat by preaching on "Stuck between the Devil and the Deep Red Sea." As I kept stirring the simmering Exodus pots, I learned principles from Moses' wilderness wanderings that helped me spiritually. I also realized the same principles were supported in the lives of friends who'd survived tough times; they have graciously allowed me to retell their stories so that their learning experiences can be yours.

Writing a book is itself a wilderness experience. I knew early in the process that I wouldn't make it without prayer. How grateful I am for those who put this project on their prayer lists—people like Dagmar, Dan, Judy, Cindy, Marie, Karen, Georgia, Peggy, Cheryl, and friends in my 1996-97 Bible Study Fellowship discussion group.

And thanks to my family—Rich, Zachary, and Inga—for hanging in there while Mom made the lonely journey through lots of rewrites. We'll now have another "stone of remembrance" for our living room memorials box (see chapter 13 for more about that)! What shall it be? Maybe a petrified French fry, for those times when Mom was stirring so vigorously on her book that Dad offered to "cook."

This is my prayer: "Open my eyes that I may see wonderful things in your law" (Ps. 119:18).

Introduction

For more months than we care to discuss, one of the main streets near our home turned into something worse than a dry riverbed. Blame ambitious builders turning nearby orchards into dozens of homes needing updated underground utility lines. Credit engineers, who agreed increased traffic required more than two much-patched, tuck-in-your-elbow lanes.

The process meant giving up our most direct route to half of the town. Instead, we wove through detours that would have frustrated even Daniel Boone. People who claimed the ripped-up street as home found that getting into their driveways aged their cars ten years in three months. Some days we woke to the growls of heavy road machinery. Some days those dinosaur scoops and rollers didn't move an inch, making us wonder how much longer we'd be streetless in Wenatchee.

Did we grumble about it? Who, us? How did you guess?

Could grumbling be something inherent in human nature? Eighteenth century English statesman Edmund Burke thought so:

> To complain of the age we live in, to murmur at the present possessors of power, to lament the past, to conceive extravagant hopes of the future, are the common dispositions of the greatest part of mankind.

There's a lot in life that's "ripe for gripes." We want things easy, quick, and convenient. We want wide, paved roads with fast speed limits on them. We want health and not disease, weight loss without exercise, family life minus its give-and-take, work that's not laborious, and homes that don't need repairs. We have the same expectations spiritually. We want the road to heaven free of life's troubles and a faith that doesn't require much of us.

But God knows zipping through life doesn't turn us into heaven-worthy people. The highway to heaven is rocky road by divine purpose. God's Word gives us a splendid illustration of this as the Israelites journeyed from Egyptian slavery to the Promised Land. As they criss-crossed the Sinai's sands for forty years, they did what we'd do: griped about it. Repeatedly they "murmured," "complained," "grumbled," and "cried out."

Not only are we just like them, but we're also to learn from them. First Corinthians 10:6 says of Israel's history: "Now these things occurred as examples to keep us from setting our hearts on evil things as they did." It can't get any plainer than that!

This book tackles those tough examples. But it also offers hope in weaving in the true stories of ordinary people who walked those spiritual rocky roads and found God alongside.

At the end of each chapter there will be "Mileposts"— questions to let you mark the progress of your own spiritual journey alone or with a group.

I don't promise a smooth road when you've finished the book. But maybe you'll understand what God is doing when he leaves the potholes there.

I am poor and needy;
may the Lord think of me.
You are my help and my deliverer;
O my God, do not delay.—Psalm 40:17

1
This Road Doesn't Go There

Despair and Hope

There must be an eleventh commandment: "Thou shalt locate Christian retreat centers in mysterious locations known only to angels and UPS drivers."

I was scheduled to speak one weekend at a camp carefully obscured in the mountain boondocks. My instructions from the retreat contact told me to turn off the highway by the tumble-down barn just past the house with butterflies on it. Check. Then she said it was "a long ways up the gravel road but you can't miss the sign." I went a long ways, and a long ways, and finally came to a Y in the road. I re-read my instructions. Nothing about a Y. The left Y looked promising, as it led past a number of houses rimming a meadow. Surely, more civilization was ahead. How was I to know that I would soon illustrate that great poem by Robert Frost about "the road not taken"? Yep, I took one less traveled by.

When the gravel road became rocks and mud, I decided to stop for help. I knocked boldly, then frantically, at someone's door.

"I'm not selling vacuum cleaners!" I hollered, hoping to

rouse them out of anonymity. They stayed hidden, probably at their real home fifty miles away.

Deciding to drive just a little farther, I found myself squishing down a one-lane trail paved with chocolate pudding. I wasn't in the mood to meet somebody coming the opposite way. As my anxiety level approached the stratosphere, my prayers went that direction, too. I decided I'd better back up before the sun completely left the sky and I'd discover new things about black holes—and not the ones in outer space.

I finally got back to my friendly Y, but the other fork looked so torn up I decided it couldn't be the way to the conference center. Heading back down the main road I encountered a car full of women headed up. I waved them to a stop.

"Ah," I said, trying to act cool and important, "you wouldn't happen to be going to the women's retreat, would you?"

"Oh yeah!" they hollered with the giddiness that descends on women liberated for their annual grown-up slumber party. "Just follow us."

After turning right at the infamous Y, they bounced over rocks big enough to slow a rhinoceros before coming to a tree-obscured sign announcing the conference center driveway. Later that weekend I did some private research about that "other road."

"I took that one time," said one woman. "I finally came to an empty logging camp way down in some gully. I almost got stuck and nearly missed the retreat."

Nutty or Nitty-Gritty?

Rocky road is not just a flavor of nutty ice cream. It's the nitty-gritty of life. It's learning that getting where we want isn't always easy. Sometimes life's journey is rutted and rocky and rough. We're not where we want to be, and yet we don't see how things can get any better.

God knows all about our despair. He's listening when we

whimper, "I can't bear it any longer." We have proof of that in the liberation of the Hebrews from Egyptian slavery, an event so epic that it has almost no equal in human history. A nation of two million people was born, ready to claim another country as its new homeland.

But this infant nation wasn't yet ready to live on its own. Neither was a boy apprehended one night behind one of our town's elementary schools. He and two friends were found with drugs and drug paraphernalia. The police took the two friends home to their parents, but, at the home of the first boy, age thirteen, they found no parent. Instead, they discovered insects crawling throughout the house and mold growing in the kitchen sink. The boy said he thought his mother was in jail in a town a hundred miles away. His father was also in jail, but he didn't know where. Left alone, he wasn't doing a very good job of taking care of himself. For his own good, he was placed in juvenile detention.[1]

God knows we need growing-up time. It's not always easy. We're apt to grumble and complain over problems that come our way. But God knows all about them. He's also watching how we respond. Bible teacher Louis Caldwell observes: "More important than what happens to us is how we react to what happens. We do have the freedom to respond to suffering in a positive way, to make it serve a purpose and give it value. Suffering can impose limits, but it cannot take away our freedom to decide what our attitudes will be."[2] God can take our negative circumstances and turn them into positive spiritual traits—if we're willing.

Our first reaction is often despair. But Exodus 1 provides us with important principles for turning despair into hope:

- Problems are no surprise to God.
- Temporary homelands seek to enslave us.
- Homesickness is *good* sickness.
- God encourages through the ordinary.
- The end of ourselves is the continuing of God.

Problems Don't Surprise God

At the end of Genesis, Jacob, his sons, and their families went to Egypt for what they thought would be a temporary relocation during the famine. They never left. For 430 years they lived and had babies who grew up and had more babies. Fearing their large numbers, a pharaoh enslaved them to gain control. Eventually slavery became so oppressive that Jacob's descendants despaired of any better future for themselves. Things were not only bad, they were getting worse.

God knew this would happen. Hundreds of years earlier he'd told Abraham: "Know for certain that your descendants will be strangers in a country not their own, and they will be enslaved and mistreated four hundred years. But I will punish the nation they serve as slaves, and afterward they will come out with great possessions" (Gen. 15:13-14).

God sees the big picture. "The eyes of the Lord are everywhere, keeping watch on the wicked and the good," says Proverbs 15:3. Some people think of God like "time bake" on an oven. They claim he set the dials and then went off. The Bible, however, says otherwise. He is omniscient—all-seeing, all-knowing: "Great is our Lord and mighty in power; his understanding has no limit" (Ps. 147:5). Nothing escapes his attention, and he knows just the right time to intervene.

I learned that from my first "rocky road" experience as a grade schooler. Mom had talked Dad into visiting her cousins, who lived in a remote village overlooking the Columbia River. From our home near Tacoma, Washington, the route by freeway took us south for 150 miles, then east for another 100 or so. Dad was not enchanted with the distance.

"Look, dear," Mom said, studying her map. "There's a road through the mountains that would cut down on the number of miles. And just think of the bee-yoo-tee-full drive it would be." She knew how to convince a Montana native who missed the Rockies. Somehow he overlooked the fact that the roads were designated with two thin lines and labeled "primitive."

As we twisted our way up into the mountains, the roads got rockier, dustier, and narrower.

"Daddy," I whimpered as I looked out of my back seat window down a dark chasm, "we're going to fall off the road. Please drive on the other side!"

"I can't," he snapped. "Somebody might come around the next bend."

A few bends later I became a candidate for a juvenile heart attack when a loud bang beneath me forced the car to a stop—right on the brink.

"Flat tire," Dad sighed as the dust settled. "Better get out of the car on the driver's side."

We soon learned that one does not attempt to change a tire in loose gravel on the down side of a drop-off. As Mom and my older sister grabbed big flat rocks to shovel "wells" securing the opposite tires, Dad frantically released the jack to keep the car from sliding farther down the shoulder.

From the "safe" side of the road, I cried and prayed in despair. On this remote mountain road, where could we get help? Where was God?

Within minutes, two vehicles with muscular drivers showed up. They helped Dad secure the car and change the tire. Did I believe God answered my prayer? You know I did! The arrival of those cars on a lonely mountain road—at just the right time—was no coincidence. God was watching.

We all at some time will experience a crisis of despair, something that tries to plunge us over the edge. I think of a friend, who within a few months experienced both life-threatening health problems and a drastic employee turnover at work. Some of us asked him, "What next?" He just smiled and said, "Hey, God's still on the throne." Even when it seems the world can't get any crazier, God knows all about it.

Temporary Homelands Enslave Us

Egypt enslaved the Israelites physically and spiritually. The physical slavery, a result of Pharaoh's fear, produced mammoth building and agricultural projects. Slaves were worked ruthlessly and their lives made bitter (Ex. 1:13-14). I've never been a slave, but I've known jobs so demanding of time and energy that I lost my joy of working. No matter how hard I worked, my employer always wanted more. I felt like a hamster trapped in an exercise wheel. Yet labor with hardship is part of life. It began when Adam and Eve sinned and were fired as caretakers of the Garden of Eden: "Cursed is the ground because of you; through painful toil you will eat of it" (Gen. 3:17). That's why we can't spend our lives lying in hammocks and sipping lemonade. Somebody has to labor to produce that lemonade.

The spiritual slavery was more subtle. Egypt shared with the Hebrews its pagan religions, and these gripped the people for generations. Even as the Hebrews stood poised to enter Canaan, Joshua had to reprimand them: "Throw away the gods your forefathers worshiped beyond the River and in Egypt" (Josh. 24:14). The idols of our age are typically built of wood, plastic, or metal, and run on electricity or gas. They entice us from the pages and screens of our media. Or they represent cravings or self-indulgent habits which put God off on the sidelines.

Homesickness Is Good Sickness

I first got homesick the second day of junior Bible camp. I cried into my pillow, then dried my tears and determined to tough out the next three days of life in an ant-infested bunkhouse with one bathroom for twenty girls. Later came college, with roommates and coursework that shattered my comfort zones. As recently as this year I got homesick when I went to a conference two states away. When I called home and heard my kids' voices—especially that of my 14 year old with his already-lowered tones—I broke down. I missed them so much!

First Peter 2:11 reminds us that we are "aliens and strangers in the world." That's a hard principle when we like our earthly homes so much. During the fifteen years between high school graduation and marriage, I had so many addresses I can't even remember all of them. I went to four colleges and held jobs in four different states. I'm sure my parents wondered if I'd ever settle down—or if I'd ever pick up the things I stored at home! The yearning of my heart was just a place to call home, where I could settle my "things" and build a future. Then I married, and I've lived in the same town and house for sixteen years now.

But there's another homesickness that's represented by the Hebrews' yearning for Canaan. For a long time I thought of the Jordan River as death and Canaan or the Promised Land as the blessedness of heaven. I grew up hearing songs like "I Am Bound for the Promised Land" and "Deep River," and hearing people refer to death as "going to the other side." But I've learned that the analogy isn't quite correct. Canaan was the site of many battles; there are no battles in heaven. Even after God's people moved in, there was much sin in Canaan, and there is nothing that defiles in heaven. Later, God's people were expelled from Canaan; once in heaven, you're there to stay.

Instead, Canaan represents the maturing Christian life. It's the physical symbol for the outworking of our new life when we "live a life worthy of the calling" we have received in Christ (Eph. 4:1). J. Oswald Sanders in *Promised Land Living* explains:

> Canaan is not heaven, but a suburb of heaven. It stands for a victorious type of Christian experience that is possible to know and enjoy here and now. . . . [It represents] the exchange of a life of defeat in the desert for the joy, rest, and fruitfulness of life in the Promised Land.[3]

We need to experience the "homesickness" that represents our deepening yearning to walk with God.

God Encourages through the Ordinary

Pharaoh's plan to kill off the Israelites through ruthless labor backfired. Their population grew. Frustrated, he decided to attack the family structure by ordering the midwives to kill off baby boys they delivered. But two ordinary women accomplished something extraordinary when they foiled his scheme. Shiphrah and Puah (whose names, respectively, mean "beauty" and "splendor") refused to follow the command, claiming that Hebrew women were vigorous and gave birth before the midwives arrived (Ex. 1:19). They felt lying to a monarch was justified when the alternative would not glorify God. All the babies they delivered lived.

Today those midwives might be called "encouragers." They're people who notice others who are down and who need the lift of a good word or deed. Lorna was such a person in my life during my first years of work. Single and in my early twenties, I faced discouragement and hardships at work, and confusing and challenging times with roommates and a boyfriend. I knew I could stop by Lorna's or call her when I needed counsel. She invited me to family dinners, helped celebrate my birthday, and made me feel important. She prayed with me. Just like those midwives, she allowed God to use her to come alongside another struggling woman.

Another picture of encouragement comes from Wrens of the British Royal Navy who helped run the shore base during the desperate days of World War II. Sailors at anchored ships kept the women's dorm under surveillance with binoculars. Realizing the women knew semaphore, some waved messages like "Hello," "How are you?" and "How about a date?" It didn't do the shipboard men much good, but they felt very dashing. The signaling was stopped on security grounds, but the men still kept watching the women. One dusk, just before the men shipped out for what would be D-Day, one woman came out of the Wren dorm and signaled just one word: Courage. Then, knowing it was against the rules, she ran back into the house.

That's what God does for us at our darkest hour. He waves, "Take courage," and sends us on.

The End of Ourselves—the Continuing of God

Exodus 1 really ends a chapter later, after the story of the baby Moses being rescued from the Nile. All during that time, the suffering people increasingly "groaned in their slavery and cried out, and their cry for help because of their slavery went up to God" (Ex. 2:23). That verse is a picture of a dark cloud, but the sun is right behind: "God heard their groaning and he remembered his covenant with Abraham, with Isaac and with Jacob. So God looked on the Israelites and was concerned about them" (Ex. 2:24-25).

To borrow a famous quote of Winston Churchill, these were not to be darker days but sterner days and great days. God was about to explode on the scene.

Long ago I saw this slogan, and I've never forgotten it: "When we come to the end of ourselves, we'll realize God was there all along." We cannot truly appreciate God's blessing until we have known despair apart from that blessing. We cannot praise his wisdom in allowing adversity until we look back and see the spiritual growth that resulted. Jerry Bridges expresses that necessity in his book *Transforming Grace:*

> It is difficult for us to see God's hand of love in the adversities and heartaches of life because we persist in thinking, as the world does, that happiness is the greatest good. Thus we tend to evaluate all our circumstances in terms of whether or not they produce happiness. Holiness, however, is a greater good than happiness. He is more concerned about our spiritual than our material welfare. So all the trials and difficulties, all the heartaches, disappointments, and humiliations come from His loving hand to make us partakers of his holiness.[4]

We want the fast route to happiness, but that will eventually lead to a ghost town. God wisely sends us off on the long road to holiness, the everlasting destination. But the journey isn't necessarily always pleasant or easy. When our family goes on a trip, we can usually count on the children whining, "Are we there yet?" about one hour into the drive. They don't want to know that there are many more hours of riding ahead. When Christians are knocked and bruised by hardship, they often demand of God, "Am I there yet? Am I holy enough yet?" Sometimes, in his mysterious wisdom, he allows things to get worse than we could have imagined. But God is still on the throne.

Someone once said, "Hope is like the sun, which, as we journey toward it, casts the shadow of our burden behind us."[5] I had to learn that as I confronted utter despair at one point in my life. When I was thirty-one and still single, my parents died six months apart—Mom of cancer and Dad of a heart attack. I dropped out of graduate school in Illinois and moved home to Washington state to settle their affairs. The "tough stuff" of death enslaved me, consuming my days as well as my emotions. I cried through everything—from sorting through their clothes and junk piles to writing notes to people who, unaware, had sent them Christmas cards.

A year later, still emotionally bruised, I returned to graduate school and finished my degree with nearly straight A's in my coursework. I thought my work and academic record would help me find a job quickly. But people in my field weren't hiring. The weeks ticked off grimly to the day I had to be out of college housing, with no place to go. I didn't even have a car—I'd left mine in Washington. Some days as I prayed through desperate tears, I wondered if God was still aware of my needs. Hope seemed irrational, yet I hoped against hope to conquer despair. I kept reading my Bible, even on days when I didn't feel like it. One day, Isaiah 61 pierced a tender spot:

> He has sent me to bind up the brokenhearted,
>   to proclaim freedom for the captives . . .
> to comfort all who mourn,
>   and provide for those who grieve in Zion—
> to bestow on them a crown of beauty

    instead of ashes,
  the oil of gladness
    instead of mourning,
  and a garment of praise
    instead of a spirit of despair.
  (Isaiah 61:1-3)

A garment of praise instead of a spirit of despair! God did care! But appropriating that promise meant endlessly saying and praying, "Okay, God, it doesn't make sense. It's tough. But you know what's best. Show me how to wait or show me what I should do. Help me to trust you and praise you as I wait." That job I trusted God for came just three heart-stopping days before the housing office deadline. And the ache of grieving eased into a quiet reminder to serve God in whatever years I had left.

I never planned on wearing rags of despair. Few of us plan lives riddled by sorrow, the pressures of work or unemployment, family or marital strife, disintegrating health, or other problems. Yet often those situations come, threatening to consume us. But God offers a hopeful alternative. He offers to exchange our rags of despair for his holy garments of praise. His garments have a designer label that reads, "Made in Heaven of New Materials." I suspect they also read, "Okay to wash in hot water" because he guarantees their durability!

God knows just the right time to break into our despair and help us. For the Israelites, the right time involved a little baby. He had to grow up, endure adolescence, and become a man of God. Pharaoh's daughter named him "Moses," because she drew him out of the water. But God also drew him up for grander purposes than the daughter of Egypt ever imagined. We'll meet him in the next chapter and learn what he had to overcome.

Mileposts

1. It's said you can measure the stature of a man by what he

grumbles about. The same is true for women. Read some of the letters to the editor in your local paper. What values do the writers seem to hold? What would be your response?

2. One of the Bible's most likely candidates for despair was Job. Read Job 13:15 for his response to incomprehensible tragedy.

3. Sometimes singing uplifting hymns and choruses can help meet the need of a despairing heart. One popular chorus is based on Psalm 42:5. If you know the tune, sing it. If not, try singing the verse to a well-known hymn, like "Amazing Grace."

4. Psalm 78 is a review of Israel's history. Skim through it and draw a little triangle (for pyramids) by the verses that speak of enslavement in Egypt.

5. Memory verse: "But you, O God, do see trouble and grief; you consider it to take it in hand" (Ps. 10:14). Other possible verses: Psalm 40:17; 54:4; 116:6; Hebrews 13:6.

My grace is sufficient for you, for my power
is made perfect in weakness.—2 Corinthians 12:9

2
Wrong Number, God!

Cowardice and Duty

I was sitting at a stoplight the other day when I noticed the drivers behind and in front of me were both talking on car phones. I wondered if they were talking to each other. So much for the back yard fence!

I've dragged my feet on conforming to this addition to the driving life. I get enough phone calls at home that give me an identity crisis. Sometimes I answer callers needing a fruit broker, the domestic crisis center, or Maria's bilingual beauty shop—all with phone numbers similar to ours. One time our number was mistakenly listed in advertising for a benefit comedy show. I know I'm not the person they want.

At times I've said the same thing to God: "Wrong number, God. I'm not the person for the job. You need somebody with lots of education or lots of talent or lots of stage presence."

But God has a way of turning us upside down and shaking all the excuses out of our pockets. Take, for example, my aversion to selling. I endured the darkest afternoons of my youth trudging door-to-door selling boxes of mints or tickets to high-school orchestra concerts. I was certain that behind each door lurked somebody who gave up candy for Lent (in October) or whose tastes were more rock than Bach. I would rather have cleaned the garage, starched Dad's shirts, or endured a root canal than sell.

My first "real" job, as a newspaper reporter, was in the same league as selling used cars. Like a salesperson, a reporter must meet people and quickly relate on a personal level, delving into their deepest feelings. Ultimately, she must convince people to let her publish these dark secrets for all the world to read. Somehow, I survived the challenge. In all my years of knocking on doors for interviews, only one dog bit me.

But selling wasn't the only skill I struggled with. There was this matter of driving. I always believed that if God intended for us to drive cars with standard transmissions, he would have created us with three arms so we could keep both hands on the wheel while manipulating the gearshift. One newspaper I worked for had a company car with—guess what?—a stick shift on the steering column.

"But I've only driven cars with automatics," I complained lamely to the managing editor as he assigned me the company car. He drew a diagram of the gear shift and warned me to take it easy on the clutch. He ignored my question about which pedal was the clutch. The whole newsroom gathered at the upstairs window overlooking the parking lot to snicker as I bucked that car like a rodeo bull. I briefly considered filing workmen's compensation for whiplash as I jerked out into traffic. But I kept trying to learn—and, eventually, I did. Years later, I actually owned a car with—yes—standard transmission.

I was starting to get the message that I can't tell God "I can't." Then he got real personal. He put his thumb on my involvement in ministry.

I'd fudged along for a few years teaching first-grade Sunday school using curriculum that provided three hours of activities for thirty minutes of teaching time. Then some older women, who'd heard that I'd been to Bible school, asked me to replace their retiring Bible-study leader.

I only invested about eighty-six hours preparing the first

study. When I arrived for the first class, my legs were so wobbly I had to sit down. My hands were swampy, so the papers kept slipping out of them. But somehow I got through it. And each week got better as I kept reminding myself, "I can do everything through him who gives me strength" (Phil. 4:13). Incredibly, the women seemed to get something out of the study. Because some had never read the Old Testament, we studied the life of David. As we got into the chapters on Bathsheba's bath, one lady in her seventies confided, "I didn't know the Old Testament could be so risqué!"

Did God overcome my reluctance? Will God overcome yours? Ask those questions of Moses, the meal the Nile's crocodiles didn't get. From Exodus 2–4 we learn some important lessons for the times when we're tempted to say, "Wrong number!"

- God must humble us before he can use us.
- You can't tell God you can't.
- When God calls us, he enables us.
- God can use all our life experiences.
- God's plans are bigger than we could possibly imagine.

God Must First Humble Us

Moses' story is a bottomless biography. Just when you think you know his story, you realize there's so much more to learn. Who would have thought that this doomed Hebrew baby would go from a precarious, floating cradle to the pretentious throne room of Egypt? As the adopted son of Pharaoh's daughter, he had every worldly advantage: education, wealth, administrative skill, and cultural finesse. He also had a bad case of arrogance. He mistakenly presumed that his adoptive status was his license to defend his birth heritage. One day he murdered an Egyptian who was beating up a Hebrew. That violent act ended his royal privilege, and he fled for his life.

Some parts of Moses' life remind me of a man who is a

leader in my community. Clyde Ballard was born in Arkansas to migrant laborers. But while Moses floated a short distance to the palace, Clyde followed his parents' long-distance searches for work. Sometimes he attended four to five different schools a year. Like Moses, he had a problem with self-control. Insecure and friendless, he became a fighter and a showoff. In high school he tried to prove himself by skipping classes, drinking, and driving wildly.

"My buddies and I crammed friends in my parents' little car and sped around corners so fast the car went sideways and the hubcaps popped off," he recalls. "One time we ignored a 'road closed' sign and shot off into a construction area, careening around huge boulders and machinery. Amazingly, we never crashed." But one night the car in which Clyde was riding *did* crash, going out of control at ninety-five miles per hour. The car started rolling, and Clyde was thrown out on the third flip and broke his shoulder. Then the rolling car crushed his foot. He recovered and continued his wild ways.

Then, at eighteen, he fell in love with a Christian girl, Ruth, and convinced her to leave college and marry him. Though marriage didn't change Clyde's wild ways, God had his hand on Clyde's life. As a child, Clyde had attended Sunday school. In his teen years, one family had taken him to church, encouraging him to make things right with God. Several of his high-school friends also had tried to tell him about being a Christian, but he put them off.

Moses put God off. For the second four decades of his life, he hid as a runaway murderer in the Midian wastelands. Routine dulled the pain of what might have been. Every morning his life focused on the survival of a bunch of sheep. But God hadn't forgotten Moses or what he wanted Moses to do. D. L. Moody once said that Moses spent forty years in Pharaoh's court thinking he was somebody. Then he spent forty years in the desert learning he was a nobody. Finally, Moses would spend forty years learning what God could do with a nobody.

The crisis came one very ordinary day, while Moses' sheep dined on dusty salad and Moses indulged in desert day-dreams. Suddenly he woke up to the miracle of a bush that burned without burning out. Then God spoke out of the bush, calling Moses by name. He told Moses to reverence his holiness by taking off his sandals. Then, God reminded Moses who he was—not a *new* god but *the* God of his ancestors.

Clyde, too, had an encounter with God. It happened one ordinary Sunday afternoon in 1956. Clyde was driving around with his friend Don, discussing the latest news about war in Israel. "Don was a minister's son, but he had rebelled," Clyde remembers. "He knew that prophecy linked Israel's woes with the end of the world. As we talked, we both realized that if Christ came that day, we wouldn't be ready."

Convicted and scared, they turned up at the door of a pastor. He took them right to the church to talk. Clyde had no problem admitting he was a sinner for whom Jesus had died. That afternoon, in an empty church, he asked Christ into his life.

You Can't Tell God You Can't

God told Moses that he'd watched the Hebrews' escalating misery for hundreds of years and was ready to rescue them. Then came the zinger: "So now, go. I am sending you to Pharaoh to bring my people the Israelites out of Egypt" (Ex. 3:10). Moses told God he'd dialed the wrong number. "Who am I?" he asked. "Who are you? Who's going to believe me? I'm not a public speaker!"

After forty years of obscurity, Moses was suffering an identity crisis. As a prince, he'd failed by trying to do God's work Moses' way. He saw himself as a fugitive, not someone holding the pedigree for leadership.

Aren't we often that way? Don't we want to say, "God, I'm not your person. I'm not important enough." Or maybe your excuses run like this: "I never went to college," "I messed up my marriage," "I did drugs," "I chose abortion." But Moses' calling shows us that God's grace is enormously encompassing. He can forgive, cleanse, and renew a murderer. Besides, if he used only sinless people, he wouldn't have anybody to do his work!

God even reached down to Clyde Ballard, which astonished his old friends. They couldn't believe how his vocabulary changed and bad habits dropped away. But there still was a lot of the "old Clyde" that took longer to change. One was materialistic ambition. He'd started working in a grocery store as a dollar-an-hour boxboy, determined to go to the top. At twenty-four, he was named general manager of the local multi-store corporation. He bought the symbols of importance: a Cadillac and a large home.

"But after I got them, I realized they didn't really satisfy me," Clyde says. "So I turned to church life and tried to be successful there. My wife and I worked with the youth group, and it grew and thrived. But I was overcommitted and spiritually empty. My pastor saw my problem and told me, but I didn't heed his warning."

Clyde kept reaching for business success. He quit the grocery business and, after a year of odd jobs, bought a used ambulance, thinking it a quick money maker. Instead, he found himself on call twenty-four hours a day and earning so little that he and Ruth had to moonlight as church janitors. They parked the ambulance outside the church in case they got an emergency call while in the middle of buffing floors.

The intensity of emergency work started to wear on their family, which now included three sons and two foster daughters. Adding an office at home eroded privacy and family time. Clyde drove himself harder and harder, expanding into a store for health-care supplies. Plus, he added the pressure of local politics, winning fire and water district races.

But while Clyde said "I can" to worldly responsibilities, he had a hard time saying "I can" to nurturing his spiritual life. "I'd drag home at night," he admits. "I knew God was allowing me all these material blessings. But I also knew my spiritual life wasn't in balance. I was too tired to read my Bible and really talk with God about where he was taking us."

Then God arranged to speak through a modern-day "burning bush"—Clyde's father.

"My father had always been an angry, argumentative man," Clyde remembers. "He knew I'd become a Christian, and others had talked to him about Christ. Then one day, working on a roof by himself, he realized how much was missing in his life. With no one around, he simply asked Christ to come into his life. We watched his attitudes toward people and life turn completely around. A little later Dad was diagnosed with cancer of the pancreas. He called his friends and relatives together and told them only Jesus Christ held the key to life's real values. He died with five dollars in his wallet and heaven's riches in his soul."

That affected Clyde as he looked at his own wealth. But God needed one more burning bush—a very big one—to really get his attention. One night at 1:20 A.M., he was awakened by a phone call from the sheriff. His business was on fire. Arson was suspected. Clyde rushed to the scene, only to watch years of work go up in smoke.

"My pastor came and sat with me in one of the ambulances parked outside the building," Clyde remembers. "He put his hand on my knee and said, 'Clyde, I want you to understand that greater things than ever before are going to come out of this situation.' "

When God Calls, He Enables

Clyde found his pastor's exhortation hard to believe. But evidence of God's hand began to accumulate almost immediately. At the height of the fire, seven 650-pound containers of liquid oxygen exploded, possibly trapping five firemen inside the building. Grabbing his two-way radio, Clyde ran to the back. Miraculously, all the men were safe. The explosion had blown them out of the building and underneath a fire truck parked in the alley.

The fire destroyed much more than Clyde's insurance

would cover. Yet as they started sifting through the rubble, they started to see the grace of God. The office was ashes, except for one just-bought fireproof cabinet holding soggy and singed—but readable—accounts receivable files.

His family struggled for five years to rebuild the business. Yet through those dark times came something money couldn't buy: countless gestures of love and care from his church family. In their loss, Clyde and Ruth found they gained far more in learning about the nature of God. Little did they know how much they'd need those lessons for his next call on their lives.

Moses, too, learned about the nature of God as he faced the burning bush. His "Who are you?" was more than the hesitant query of a scared-stiff shepherd. Four hundred years of slavery had left his people with only a fading oral history of God's previous intervention in their lives. Four decades of aloneness had left Moses spiritually empty, too.

God's cryptic reply—"I AM WHO I AM" (Ex. 3:14)—says more than we think at first. The original Hebrew implies God's incomprehensible greatness. Nothing caused him. No imagination invented him. He just is. He is personal, ready to reveal who he is. He's I AM, not "I was." In choosing I AM to express his essence to Moses, God used the same Hebrew word as *I will be,* as in "I will be with you." The implication was that God would reveal more of himself to Moses and the Hebrews as history unfolded.

That same I AM is a stumbling block for many people who don't take Christian faith seriously. It's not surprising. In spite of all that God has shown us, in spite of his invasion in history as Jesus Christ, there are still people who hang onto the lie that God is dead. It's their problem, not God's: "For since the creation of the world God's invisible qualities—his eternal power and divine nature—have been clearly seen, being understood from what has been made, so that men are without excuse" (Rom. 1:20). When we're without excuse, we're helpless under the glare of God.

Yet, we still try our excuses. Moses' next one—"Who's

going to believe me?"—dealt with his credibility. He didn't think anybody would listen to him. Even after God arranged for Moses to perform a series of miracles before the Hebrew elders and Pharaoh, Moses still doubted his calling as God's leader.

So many times we're like Moses: afraid of failure. But when we fear trying because we fear losing, or when we let others discourage us, we set ourselves up for failure. Yet the discouragers aren't always right.

- A Boston music critic said in 1837, "If Beethoven's Seventh Symphony is not by some means abridged, it will soon fall into disuse."

- Simon Newcomb declared in the 1800s, "Flight by machines heavier than air is impractical and insignificant—utterly impossible."

- A Munich schoolmaster told ten-year-old Albert Einstein, "You will never amount to very much."[6]

- Forty-two publishers rejected a children's fantasy book by Madeleine L'Engle before one took on *A Wrinkle in Time,* which then received the Newbery Medal for excellence in children's fiction.

God Uses All Our Life Experiences

While Moses continued to label himself a failure, God saw the big picture. God knew very well who Moses was. God had tailored him uniquely in urban and rural settings. The city man could manage people and administer law and had dabbled in arts, crafts, and other skills of highly civilized people. The country man knew how to survive in the uninhabitable places, find water, care for flocks, and cope with boredom. He'd need both sets of skills to lead thousands around Sinai for forty years.

God knows all about us, too. He created our minds, programmed our bodies, and allowed the circumstances that made us who we are. We're mosaics of education, culture, travel, friends, family, successes, and even failures. Under his creative hand, the tiles come together to fit his purpose. I don't have to look any further than the mirror for validation!

Just out of college, I wondered what God could do with all the classes I took in English, journalism, and music—especially when my first job involved writing police news, obituaries, and headlines for recipes. But God allowed this breadth of experience to help me become a more versatile writer and speaker. He used my numerous nerve-racking interviews to help me develop social skills. He put me in less-than-perfect office situations to build my patience. And he used all the disciplines of music (oh, those back-breaking hours practicing the violin!) to build the discipline needed for being self-employed.

For Clyde, too, the time would come when he'd know how God would use his mistakes as a scrappy youth. He'd be able to apply the business acumen he had acquired from struggling to succeed with just a high-school education. He'd know why God kept pulling him back to the basics of his faith, even using a fire that destroyed everything he'd worked for. In 1982, Clyde felt God calling him to make a difference through state government. He won the state representative race from his district in central Washington. At the end of his first term he was elected caucus chairman. In his next term, he became house minority leader. By his seventh term in 1995, when his party held the majority, he took the gavel as Speaker of the House, the second most powerful man in Washington state government.

God's Plans Are Bigger Than Big

All of us are like Moses in that we're just human vessels through which God can work. Clyde realizes this acutely as a Christian legislator whose every word and decision comes under special scrutiny. "My testimony is continually on display," says Clyde, whom political writers have nicknamed "Mr. Rogers" for his gentle demeanor. "People watch how you act under pressure, after long hours and in conflicts, because government is basically a place of conflict."

Clyde's position would probably have overwhelmed Moses, the ragtag prince-turned-shepherd who argued with God. Moses' last excuse shows how much he wanted out of the job God planned for him: "I have never been eloquent, neither in the past nor since you have spoken to your servant. I am slow of speech and tongue" (Ex. 4:10).

I can identify with Moses' excuse that he was a "bumblemouth." When I get up to speak, fear turns my throat into the Sahara desert and my brain shifts into neutral. That's why I need to cover my inadequacies with prayer that God will use me in spite of my weaknesses.

Our human inabilities are only a problem when we refuse to turn them over to God. When Moses complained about his speaking ability, God reluctantly assigned his brother Aaron as a spokesman. But Aaron wasn't God's first choice. Aaron had spent all his life in the midst of Egypt's idolatry. Aaron was such a smooth talker that he'd later lead the Hebrews into worshiping a golden calf, right at the base of the mountain where Moses was getting the Ten Commandments from the very hand of God.

Clyde knows well the vulnerability of leadership. He keeps strong ties to his home church, often leading a Sunday school class there. For the majority of his years in the state capital, he's taken leadership for Christian outreach, including Bible study groups and the Governor's Prayer Breakfast. He's also serious about his own prayer life, knowing the issues he faces in government are often Satan's veiled attempts to destroy God's plan for families and community.

"Sometimes Ruth and I laugh because God is stretching us so far beyond our human abilities," Clyde says. "My mixed-up background of poverty and success has helped me relate to those who have little materially as well as to prominent businessmen. God's also placed me before foreign rulers and our own president and vice president. With many, we've been able to talk about the Lord."

Clyde considers Matthew 6:33 his life verse: "Seek ye first the kingdom of God, and his righteousness; and all these things shall be added unto you" (KJV). "I used to be obsessed with seeking success in business," he says, "then God took it away. He showed me that success comes through knowing Jesus Christ. When I seek him and his righteousness, then he adds good things. For me, it's been the privilege of serving as our state's Speaker of the House, influencing the lives of millions. I'm a living example of how God can use a nobody to accomplish his work in high places."

When you're an instrument in God's hand, reluctance is not an option. God calls us to duty. Excuses fall before him. Poverty? Clyde knew it, so did Moses. Wealth? Yes, both again. Fame? Obscurity? Yes, yes. But when God calls a man, God grooms him, not dooms him. When God calls a woman, God raises her up. He doesn't knock her down. "For I know the plans I have for you," God says, "plans to prosper you and not to harm you, plans to give you hope and a future" (Jer. 29:11).

Sometimes the journey to that hope and future is a road rutted with fear. As we follow Moses back to the palace, we'll find out just how rutted it is.

Mileposts

1. Moses wasn't the only murderer God used in ministry. Read Acts 7:57-8:3, then 1 Timothy 1:15-16. What happened between the two texts? How can you identify with the passage in 1 Timothy?
2. None of Moses' life experiences were wasted. Read Ezekiel 22:30 and think through how the palace and poverty prepared Moses to "stand in the gap." Is there a negative in your life that God can turn into a positive?
3. Most of us can identify with Moses' excuse that he was not

a public speaker. Yet all of us are called to speak for the Lord; when we do, people will listen. Think about yesterday. What did people hear from you? Criticism, nagging, complaining, gossip? Or kindness, praise, encouragement? Read Proverbs 12:18; James 1:26; and 1 Peter 3:10.

4. Moses accepted God's commission because he had a vision of God. But notice: that vision came on an ordinary day. Sometimes we expect God to grab our attention only at some retreat or conference. What does Proverbs 8:34 say about appointments with God? What's a practical way to work that out?

5. Memory verse: "The fear of others lays a snare, but one who trusts in the LORD is secure" (Prov. 29:25, NRSV).

He divided the sea and led them through;
he made the water stand firm like a wall.—Psalm 78:13

3

Stuck between the Devil and the Deep Red Sea

Fear and Fortitude

Long ago I used to believe that the shortest distance between two points was the back road that hardly anybody knew about. That was during my young, brash days as the *Wenatchee World*'s Lois Lane—intrepid, fresh-from-college, girl reporter, ready to jump entire courthouses with a single bound.

Then came my day of reckoning, a bitter winter afternoon when my assignments in the hinterlands had run late and I just wanted to get home. Instead of risking the icy curves in Pine Canyon, I headed for the loop through Badger Mountain. All went well until I came to the unofficial uphill Badger Mountain ice rink. In true championship tradition, my car put its double axles in the ditch. Naturally, I was wearing a lightweight coat and no boots. *Well, Lord,* I muttered, *have I got myself into a fix.* I figured it was a three-mile walk through the snow to the nearest house.

I hadn't gone more than a hundred feet when one of the most beautiful vehicles in the world rounded the corner. I'm not talking Rolls Royce; I'm talking snow plows. Specifically, snow plows driven by muscular, capable men who like to work hard for our tax dollars.

Being stuck somewhere with an incapacitated car is only one of the life situations that upset me. Swimming is another. The college I went to was chosen for its strong music program. I was unaware that graduation required passing a swimming test. I didn't swim. In fact, I had always feared deep water. I was the child who always clung to the edge of the pool, fully buoyant in my neon-orange life jacket. Stepping into a boat put me into adrenaline overdrive. So here I was at college, age eighteen, garbed in a black, college-issue swimsuit that hung on me like a funeral drape, quivering in a line of freshmen slated for the Great Fearsome Swimming Test.

Thankfully, the water at the shallow end was waist deep. As I plunged in and showed the instructor my flailing Dutch windmill stroke, she didn't bother suggesting I try the deep end. Swimming 101, here I come. I had ten weeks to go from phobia to proficiency. The final test—diving into the deep end, treading water, then four laps across the Olympic-size pool—seemed impossible. But God reminded me, "Is anything too hard for the Lord?" (Gen. 18:14). I passed. Not with a stellar performance, but it was good enough to satisfy the lady with the clipboard. Chalk it up as another defeat for the grumble that goes, "I can't."

Yet "I can't" was surely on Moses' mind as he trudged back to Egypt to face the new pharaoh with an incredible demand. Moses knew he couldn't say "I can't" anymore. God had made it very clear that the almighty, wise, eternal I AM WHO I AM would help Moses do what God wanted. But fear still sneered.

Exodus 5–15 is full of lessons from the many times God had to deal with Moses' negative attitude. Among them:

- Fear causes us to give up easily.
- Fear reveals what we think of God's power.
- Overcoming fear requires a willingness to obey.
- God knows what's behind us and what's before us.

Fear and Giving Up

As he prepared his first inaugural address in 1933, President Franklin D. Roosevelt saw a nation discouraged and wrung out by the Depression. Many, remembering a world war fifteen years earlier, warily watched Japanese aggression in China and the rising movement called Nazism in Germany. The new president attempted to shore up the nation's courage with this memorable line: "The only thing we have to fear is fear itself."

Some fears are good. Fear of dangerous situations—like falling, fire, or wild water—encourages our safety. But many fears paralyze us instead of teaching us to team up with God. For example, fear of failure causes us to procrastinate or to not start at all. I put off cleaning the garage. Others avoid yard work or organizing their closets. Some put off dieting. Exercising. Writing thank you letters. Visiting the elderly. Asking forgiveness. Reading the Bible. Witnessing.

It's easy to understand Moses' complaint when he bumped into fear as soon as he went to bat for God. When he stepped to the plate to ask Pharaoh to release the Israelites for a religious holiday in the desert, Pharaoh responded with strike one: "Why are you taking the people away from their labor? Get back to your work!" (Ex. 5:4). Just as quickly came strike two: Pharaoh accused the Israelites themselves of laziness. As punishment, they'd now have to find their own straw and make just as many bricks as before. Then, strike three: the Israelites turned on Moses. Moses was ready to hide in the dugout. To paraphrase Exodus 5:22-23: "I thought I was supposed to deliver my people. But it's gone from bad to worse. Pharaoh wouldn't listen and the people are more miserable than ever!"

My friends Stan and Wendy Smoke experienced similar dismay when they sensed God's call to a very special ministry of deliverance. Their story began one fall day in 1990 when Stan, a firefighter (yes, he's teased about his last name), took his wife and three children along when he attended an out-of-town seminar.

While surfing the channels of the motel television, they stopped at a documentary about the estimated 100,000 Romanian children living in squalid orphanages. Daughter Amber, then thirteen and needing a country to study for her home-schooling curriculum, was gripped by the story. So were the rest of the family as they learned of former dictator Nicolae Ceausescu's obsession with increasing Romania's population. Before his 1989 assassination, he'd outlawed birth control and ordered every married woman to bear at least five children. With an average monthly income of $50, many were forced to turn their babies over to state orphanages.

Years before, when Stan and Wendy's finances were lean, they'd decided their family was complete with three. Later, they'd talked casually about adoption. But the television show propelled their "maybe" into a determined quest to bring two Romanian orphans into their family.

Piles of paperwork followed as they worked through a Christian adoption agency. Because adoptive parents were required to live in Romania for a month, many mothers were going there alone. But Wendy felt she needed Amber along—for practical help and support, as well as to provide her an education no book could offer. Yet, the closer they got to their goal, the more problems threatened its success.

"I had to turn to God over and over," Wendy says. "One thing after another threatened to shut the process down after all our plans and dreams and investment. It seemed to climax just days before our flight out. I fell down the basement stairs and thought at first I'd broken my ankle. It turned out to be just a bad sprain, and I was able to hobble onto the airplane. We also lacked some critical documents which arrived just the day before we left."

Our Fears Versus God's Power

God will often allow disappointments so he can better showcase his power in bringing about the very best. Moses suffered his own setbacks. His impasse with Pharaoh took extra effort because it was a cosmic battle between the Lord of the universe and the gods of the Egyptians. To prove the Egyptian gods worthless, God tailored ten plagues to undermine the authority of specific Egyptian deities.

#1—Turning the Nile into blood (some say this meant a reddish mess of dirt and algae), an insult to the main god of the Nile plus lesser gods for the Nile's sources, essence, and fish. We who grow up with clean water cannot imagine the devastation the fouled Nile brought to daily life.

#2—Frogs, to ridicule the frog goddess worshiped for fertility and help in childbirth. Even Pharaoh had frogs between his sheets. When that plague ended, the stench of rotted frogs gagged everybody. And my family thinks our kitchen garbage bin gets bad during canning season!

#3—Gnats, polluting the pagan temples and bringing shame to the earth deity. I'm no great fan of the insect world, having survived critters in the flour (protein-enhanced biscuits, coming up!), head lice on camp outs (how do you delouse a tent?), and hornets playing peek-a-boo in the family room blinds, but spare me wall-to-wall gnats!

Then God sent plagues affecting only the Egyptians. Flies (#4) insulted some of the insect gods. A disease on livestock (#5) attacked worship of animal and animal-headed deities. Boils from strewn ashes (#6) ridiculed the practice of priests "blessing" the people with ashes. Hail (#7) showed the worthlessness of the sky gods. Locusts (#8) attacked the goddess of grain, the guardian of fields, and the deity of harvests. Darkness (#9) was an affront to the sun god Ra, one of the chief deities.

Today, the plagues teach us that God can arrange circumstances to strike down any little idol we put up for ourselves.

It may be trust in our self-sufficiency, organization, reputation, wealth, education, or anything else that detracts from God's power. Wendy found that true as she and Amber arrived in Bucharest and began a month-long battle with bureaucracy, corruption, missed appointments, and broken promises.

"I tend to have a take-command, efficiency-oriented personality," says Wendy. "But this process left me helpless. I had no choice but to let God work things out." The Smokes had planned for two Romanian children; their adoption contact, Florentina, said they'd only get one, and she'd need more money for even that one.

The boy chosen for the Smokes—the second child of a single, impoverished woman—had lived since six months of age in an orphanage three hours' drive from Bucharest. Arriving there, Wendy couldn't locate her adoption contact. Officials didn't remember seeing her either. Worse, they were too late to start papers that day. Then Florentina drove up with the little child she'd persuaded the orphanage to release, against the rules.

Wendy peered into the dirty back seat of Florentina's car and saw her new son for the first time. He wore three sets of clothes and an old, pink, knitted cap. He sank into Wendy's lap and sighed, his dark eyes full of fear. This wasn't how Wendy envisioned adopting a child, anymore than the Hebrews expected freedom to cost such tremendous physical suffering.

"He looked too old for two and a half," Wendy remembers. "Later, we learned he was bloated from being force-fed bread and potatoes at the orphanage. He had chronic diarrhea. He also screamed when we tried to bathe him. His orphanage 'baths' had consisted of workers splashing cold water on the children. At night, he'd rock himself on his bed, seeking comfort."

The worst was yet to come. After a long month in a cramped, rented room, Wendy learned that officials had canceled their final court date.

Fear and Obeying God

Wendy struggled through Romania's archaic phone system to communicate an urgent prayer request to her family in the States. God heard: she was able to get another court date before their flight out on nonrefundable tickets. But her day in court to adopt Andrew would prove to be one of the hardest days of her life.

"I rode three hours in a dirty, smoky car to the courthouse in Andrew's town," she remembers. "Then I sat for seven bone-chilling hours on a wooden bench next to Andrew's mother in the unheated courtroom foyer."

Just half an hour before Wendy's appointment, her adoption contact backed out of representing her. Through tears, the contact explained that the Romanian government might pass a law retroactively punishing paid adoption contacts. Wendy's heart sank. Would she fail to get Andrew's release—after all this? Was God still in control?

The same questions hung in the Hebrews' hearts as God revealed his final plague. He sent an angel of death to strike dead every firstborn son, including Pharaoh's. This judgment crushed Egypt's belief that Pharaoh and his son were divine.

It's hard to imagine the terror in the land that night. A couple of years ago I rented Cecil B. DeMille's classic *The Ten Commandments* to help my children understand the Old Testament stories. Although the movie is not a model of biblical accuracy, it did evoke one key emotion: the awe, fear, and chill on Passover night as the angel of death wound its way through Egypt.

One thing was different about this plague. It would pass over Hebrew homes that participated in a specific, though strange, rite. Hebrew families were to slaughter a perfect lamb at twilight and smear its blood on their door frames. Then they were to roast the meat over a fire, eat it in haste with bitter herbs and unleavened bread, and wait. All the other plagues had been spectator events. This one required

47

them to be participants, to obey commands they did not understand.

The Bible doesn't tell us how many people failed to follow through on the Passover instructions. I would imagine very few didn't. By now they had seen enough of God's power and wrath to know there would be serious consequences for ignoring him. That night they waited in the gloomy corners of their poor homes as the specter of death crept over the marked homes to strike the Egyptians. By morning, the hopeless wails of grieving Egyptians affirmed that God was the mighty God. He had honored his people's obedience.

God Knows the "Behind" and the "Before"

As the Hebrews left the land of slavery, they marched right into another test. Behind them pressed their old life, in the form of Pharaoh's pursuing soldiers. The loss of thousands of firstborn males and all his slave labor left Pharaoh with a precarious hold on the throne. He needed those slaves back! And it looked like he might get them: the Hebrews' short journey had put them at a dead end on the shores of the Red Sea. No bridges, no ferries—talk about being trapped between the devil and the deep Red Sea!

Yet this is the very arena in which many Christians live. They've known the joy of salvation, the incredible release from a painful past, and the hope of something better ahead. They want to move forward with God, to dare and do great things with him. But right on the edge of its happening, they find themselves stuck between the old life with its enslavements and the place where God will test their newfound faith.

When you're hemmed in by circumstances, it's easy to lose perspective. Listen to the Hebrews' panic:

> Was it because there were no graves in Egypt that you brought us to the desert to die? What have you done to

us by bringing us out of Egypt? Didn't we say to you in Egypt, "Leave us alone; let us serve the Egyptians"? It would have been better for us to serve the Egyptians than to die in the desert! (Ex. 14:11-12)

Think about it. They never told Moses to leave them alone so they could serve the Egyptians. They could hardly wait to get out from under the oppression! Their negative reactions could be traced to several things. For one, not all who left Egypt were Hebrews. Exodus 12:38 says "many other people went up with them." These were hangers-on who didn't embrace the Hebrews' God, but who were awed by the plagues and saw this as their chance to leave. The Hebrews also had no scriptures to help them understand God's ways; all this was new to them. Finally, as slaves, they'd lived so long on the edge of survival that they easily reacted with fear.

When we're faced with a step of faith, we're often tempted to react like the Hebrews. We're skeptical, selfish, stubborn, and shortsighted. We tend to think of what used to be, not what can be. Sometimes unbelieving friends encourage us to doubt. We may not know what the Bible says about God's power, or we choose to ignore it, or the situation brings us so close to bare survival that we wonder if God has forgotten us. But we still need to do what God told the Hebrews: Let go, look up, and launch out.

Let Go

"Do not be afraid," Moses told the people (Ex. 14:13a). God knows how prone we are to fear our circumstances. When things get tough—in our jobs, marriages, even our churches—we tend to want to run away. He knew the Hebrews were in a cul-de-sac. He planned it that way so they couldn't take any credit for their deliverance! When God allows us to be hemmed in, he's just setting the stage for his miracle.

Look Up

"Stand firm and you will see the deliverance the Lord will bring you today" (Ex. 14:13b). All the Hebrews could see was the dust from the wheels of Pharaoh's approaching chariots. God was saying, "Don't look at the landscape, look at me!" When God takes us beyond our ability to solve something, we're on the edge of seeing something fantastic. "The Lord will fight for you; you need only to be still," Moses said (v. 14). The hardest part of a faith-building experience is waiting for God to act. But he will do it.

Launch Out

"Then the Lord said to Moses, 'Why are you crying out to me? Tell the Israelites to move on'" (v. 15). God wasn't going to leave them sitting in the sand. He dropped his blinding pillar of cloud right over the Egyptian pursuers, called up a wind to clear a road through the sea, and sent the Hebrews through. Never could they have imagined this solution to their problem! But God knew just what he would do.

Someone once said, "God delivers us not so much out of hardships as through them." Wendy experienced that as she grappled with the adoption contact's last-minute withdrawal. She went ahead with her only option: hiring a local lawyer on the spot. After the hearing, she faced one more wrenching experience. Andrew's birth mother insisted Wendy meet her parents.

"I gave them an extra passport picture of Andrew," she remembered. "They stared at it intently, then placed it carefully on the family bookshelf. Despite the language barrier, I sensed the love they felt for this child their daughter couldn't support. How much I wanted to assure them that our family would love him just as much."

God's timing was right. Wendy and Amber flew home with Andrew just one day before the Romanian government clamped down on foreign adoptions.

The Red Sea Revisited

> When the past is immobilizing,
> the present looks impossible,
> and the future looks impassable,
> God is still imperturbable.

We show our belief when God sends an "impossible" situation into our lives. For Wendy, it was her dream of adopting a second child Andrew's age, since their "home-grown" family consisted of three teenagers.

The Smokes pursued adoption possibilities in two other Eastern European countries. Twice they came home empty-handed. Then they learned of Max, a three and a half year old in an orphanage in northern Russia. This time they saw Max ahead of time, via a video from the orphanage. And this time, Stan planned to accompany Wendy to adopt Max. But the day before leaving, they got crushing news: "Don't come."

"It felt like I'd experienced a miscarriage," says Wendy. "They gave no reason for canceling the adoption. I was angry, hurt, confused. We had thought God was in this process. Now we wondered how he could allow this setback to happen. I didn't know whether I should pray for God to keep opening the door to adopt Max or whether I should take the circumstances as evidence the door was closing."

Within two weeks they learned the reason for the cryptic denial. Max's mother had refused to appear in court to sign papers relinquishing him. The adoption agency had to then prove abandonment. Holidays brought further delays. But Max was still adoptable. When the okay finally came, Wendy and Stan had to revise all their diplomatic paperwork. But within five days they were waiting in the hall at Max's orphanage.

"I thought we'd finally gotten through the Red Sea," says Wendy. "Finally, there would be no more battles or frustrations."

She was wrong. The docile child they saw in the video had a fighter spirit. When something displeased him, he yelled, spit, and butted his head into Wendy's face so hard her lips bled.

"I saw this horrible side of him just a day before we were to officially adopt him," Wendy recalls. "Stan and I wondered what we were getting into. Were we taking on more than we could handle? Would this child fit into our settled home?"

But they also saw a tender side to him, possibly overwhelmed by all that was happening. The next day they completed the paperwork, checked him out of the orphanage, and rushed to the airport to start the long trip home.

"In Moscow the next day, he again hit my face. Then he saw some children playing outside and yelled what our translator said were obscenities. Right away I said, 'Talk nice,' then added with a pleasant voice as a model, 'Hi, children!' When he got rough, I looked him in the eye and told him in Russian, 'No, be gentle to Mama.' Then I took his hand and put it gently on my face. After that he was rough only one or two times. Each time I gave him that replacement behavior. Now he touches my face all the time, but always gently. That drastic change of behavior was like God parting the Red Sea and affirming that this child was, indeed, the one for us."

Today, Andrew and Max are well-fed, well-mannered, well-groomed, and especially well-loved little boys with ready hugs. They have a future full of the opportunities that America offers them. How different it would have been had Wendy and Stan complained, "We can't make it, Lord. The obstacles are too big. We're afraid of the bureaucracy and the unknowns."

But the Smokes faced their Red Seas with the courage that comes from believing God goes before them. When they didn't see the solutions to seemingly insurmountable problems, he took them through in ways that caused people to agree, "The Lord led."

Sometimes, even after we experience God's deliverance, we forget where our strength and hope come from. We'll see that in the next chapter.

Mileposts

1. It is difficult to read the Passover story in Exodus 12 without thinking of Jesus Christ, whom John called "the Lamb of God, who takes away the sin of the world" (John 1:29). The Hebrews had to trust God that the sign of lamb's blood would spare their homes from death. How does this relate to Jesus' mission of dying on the cross? Read Hebrews 9:14 and 1 Peter 1:18-19. What does the blood of Christ mean to you personally?

2. The Hebrews were told to celebrate the Passover meal every year as a reminder of their miraculous deliverance. How do you remember your personal spiritual victories? One person gives a new penny to a new Christian, telling her or him that the date on the coin will be a reminder of the date of his or her spiritual birth. Another uses a page in his Bible to record his spiritual history. Still another celebrates two birthdays—one for being born and one for being "born again." What could you do?

3. When people today are ecstatically happy, they are apt to jump, clap, or throw "high-fives." The Hebrews celebrated their joy with the song in Exodus 15:1-18. Read it and then go back to verse 13. The word translated "love" or "mercy" is a Hebrew word, *chesed,* which has no satisfactory equivalent in English. It describes a relationship embracing loyalty, steadfastness, mercy, and love. What other words can you think of to describe God's love?

4. The Red Sea is a place of victory, but it is also a warning. Read 1 Corinthians 10:1-13 and decide what keeps many Christians from fully knowing the blessings God planned for them. Is one of these a problem area for you? What steps would God have you take to overcome this problem?

5. Memorize this promise for times when you face a Red Sea crisis: "When you pass through the waters, I will be with you; and when you pass through the rivers, they will not sweep over you" (Isa. 43:2a).

*Call me Mara, because the Almighty has made
my life very bitter.—Ruth 1:20*

4
Going the Wrong Way on a
One-Way Street

Bitterness and Forgiveness

One of the dumbest things I ever did, I did on a one-way street. Just after I married, my eyes still starry with "newlyweditis," I had an errand downtown. Although I'd been away from town for eight years, I felt I still remembered my way around. I headed down First Street and turned right onto Mission Street. Soon I realized I was headed into Mission Impossible, for the signal a block down had just turned green and 5,806 cars (give or take 5,800) were headed my way, in all three lanes. Fortunately, I was able to back up to the corner and navigate to my destination via a more "traffically correct" route.

There was another time when my ignorance put a feline life on the line. It was summer in the mid-1950s and my mother had taken my older sister and me from Southern California's smog for a fresh-air break in North Dakota. Mom had grown up just over the border in Montana, in a town named Savage, and she was overdue for a visit with extended family. While the adults sat and gabbed, I did what eight-year-old city slickers tend to do: nose around. Everything was new and interesting, including this little roofed box between the farm house and the barn. It was too low for a doghouse, so I concluded it was haven to the tribe of kittens chasing each others' tails. I scooped up a likely candidate and pushed it through the little hole on one side.

I don't remember a whole lot after that—except there was a splash, a desperate meow, and a commotion while the farm cousins went after kitty. Oh, the jokes afterward about how cousin Jeanne gave the nursery rhyme about "kitty in the well" a whole new meaning. And all those remarks about contaminated well water! How was I to know? Where I lived, water came from faucets. Ever since then, when I've tasted bad water, I've remembered poor kitty swimming for all of her nine lives.

I can understand the Hebrews' first frustration after the Red Sea. They'd stepped into the Sinai desert with their adrenaline in overdrive. The bodies of Pharaoh's soldiers and horses still floating on the sea, they'd stopped to express the inexpressible: that God is God, and there is no other God as powerful as he. The first half of Exodus 15 tells how Miriam, Aaron's sister and a prophet in her own right, led the people in song, exclaiming, "Sing to the Lord, for he is highly exalted. The horse and its rider he has hurled into the sea" (v. 21).

Three days later they forgot that song. God had led them through the waters, but now they had no water. Without water, you die. Without water, their story would end.

Imagine their elation when they found a little well. But the first taste-testers found it bitter, perhaps so heavily loaded with mineral deposits or microorganisms that it was completely unpalatable. This is where important lessons came out concerning their own attitudes of bitterness:

- Life offers many opportunities to be bitter.
- Bitterness grows from a short memory of the good, a long memory of the bad.

- Bitterness is a whole family of sins.
- A bitter spirit loses its foulness at the cross of Jesus Christ.
- God can lead us to sweeter waters.

Many Opportunities to Be Bitter

Babies will try anything at least once. So it was that toddler Zach grunted for a slice of lemon I'd served along with fish that evening. One chew and his face exercised all its muscles. I wish I'd had the camera handy! He discovered that lemons were definitely not oranges.

Life offers lots of lemons. Even situations that look good on the outside have their bitterness. How accurate that hippie song of the sixties—that the pretty lemon tree has fruit that's impossible to eat! In the Hebrews' case, a spring that looked good left them gagging instead of satisfied.

Fouled pools exist in other areas of life. I think of the experience of someone I'll call Lynn. She loved her work at a church-sponsored preschool. Gentle, firm, loving, and steady, she had many parents request their children be placed in her class. Then one cool November day, just after Lynn finished matching children to waiting rides, the minister asked her to come to the school office. There she heard the church board's chairman dismiss her by stating, "You're no longer needed on staff."

"Why?" she asked, incredulous.

"The board has made that decision," he replied, refusing to elaborate. "Clean your room of your belongings. We'll have a check ready when you leave."

That was it. No evaluation. No two-week notice. No farewell party. No expressions of appreciation.

Dazed and unbelieving, Lynn returned to her room, crying as she looked around. Taking her supplies would leave it empty. She couldn't bear to let the children return to a bare room. Yet the minister and board chairman refused to let her leave her things until the end of the year.

Numbly, she loaded a pickup with her teaching supplies and drove away from a decade-long chapter of her life. Parents and friends were shocked and confused as the news rippled out. There was no evidence of wrongdoing or crime. Her dismissal seemed arbitrary and harsh. The place that had brought Lynn so much refreshing satisfaction was now fouled by rejection.

A Short Memory of the Good

When someone or something hurts us, all we can think about is our wound. One day I didn't navigate well and put my foot on a collision course with a door frame. For more than a week, all I could think about was my broken little toe. I forgot about the decades I had walked around with all toes in working order. Instead, I grumbled about my temporary debilitation. That's just what the Hebrews did when they found bitter water at the place called Marah. Exodus 15:24 says, "The people grumbled against Moses, saying, 'What are we to drink?'"

"Grumbled" here doesn't mean the type of moaning and groaning my kids pull when they don't like the dinner menu. The grumbles here were like a tidal wave. They started with a little discontent and then got bigger and bigger before they finally crashed on the authority figure, Moses.

This wasn't the first time the Hebrews had complained. They'd sung "Woe is me" for several hundred years, and their chorus got even louder as God began setting the stage for their liberation. The Bible records this and other grumbling incidents for a purpose: "These things happened to them as examples and were written down as warnings for us, on whom the fulfillment of the ages has come" (1 Cor. 10:11).

We're so much like the Hebrews. When life turns against us, we easily lapse into bitterness. We may pout or snap back. We might cut ourselves off from God by slacking off in prayer or Bible reading. Or we may let bitterness simmer, becoming miserable to be around.

The point of Marah was not the chemistry of the water. It was the Hebrews' refusal to trust the God who'd already brought them far. They had a short memory of the past. Of course God hadn't abandoned them. But when you're in the midst of pain, it's easy to lose sight of God's purposes.

That was Lynn's experience as she sorrowfully emptied her room. She tried to guess the board's reasoning, since they refused to give her any explanation. She wondered if her decision to attend a church of another denomination offended the leaders of this denominationally oriented church school. She thought about the time the new minister came by and remarked that the school would be better when she left and the school was no longer seen as "Lynn's school." His thoughtless remark had some truth to it. Lynn had essentially started the school, but she did so at the request of a previous minister who saw her gifts for early-childhood education.

Lynn was among nine mothers who opened their community's first preschool. Later, her home became another preschool. When severe migraine headaches struck, Lynn's doctor advised her to quit both her work and church involvement. But her minister pleaded with her to start a preschool at the church, using her nine former students as a nucleus. When no teacher could be found, Lynn felt God calling her to teach—and she never missed a day of school because of headaches.

The school prospered, growing to more than a hundred students in preschool and kindergarten with several teachers. Lynn loved her work and knew she was in God's place of ministry. Then her dream died.

After her dismissal, caring people sent cards or brought flowers. Their expressions reminded Lynn of a funeral. Each morning she woke to the depressing reminder that she wouldn't be going to school; she'd never see her students again.

Confusion and anger warred inside her as she struggled to react in a way that would honor God. It was difficult to accept that her abrupt dismissal came at the hands of those who also professed to follow the Lord. She turned a basement corner of her home into a "quiet room," where she prayed and searched Scripture for comfort and hope. "When my soul felt its darkest," she recalls, "I'd play tapes of praise songs and sing at the top of my voice. I could only trust that praise would replace my mourning."

It wasn't easy. She was told she was no longer welcome at that church, not even to attend weddings or funerals. "Sometimes, when I saw the minister at the shopping mall, I'd tremble in anger," she confesses. "He'd turn his head to avoid seeing me. As my mind replayed the dismissal, sometimes my anger returned in agonizing intensity. I even prepared a letter to the board members, expressing my hurt and challenging them to reveal the truth to the congregation. But I never sent the letter."

The Bitterness Family

Bitterness is not an isolated emotion. It's a sin that invades all our being. Let's say someone hurts our feelings or offends us. Maybe they keep grating on a pet peeve. Or maybe they violate our "rights." If our response is tinged with bitterness, people will pick up on it. Our eyes, our actions, the inflection of our voices, as well as the very words we use to describe the situation, will reveal how much we choose to forgive—and, thereby, obey and honor God.

My children have taught me a lot about this. They have a quarrel, and soon they're steaming behind their separate, closed doors. Each is too proud to admit he or she may be a part of the problem. Enter Mom, the referee. I mentally flip a coin to decide which child to approach first. Finally, I have them meet in the hall between their rooms for that vital "I'm sorry, will you forgive me?" exchange. The apology is usually quite wooden, and the compulsory hug-each-other conclusion reminds me of old-time cigar store statues. I wonder what I'm achieving with this exercise, except building in them a reminder that they need to settle differences before they get out of hand and allow anger and bitterness to ruin relationships.

The Bible is clear: bitterness is a sin with many ugly expressions. The Amplified Bible helps us understand the force of the Greek words the apostle Paul used in Ephesians 4:31 to explain it: "Let all bitterness and indignation and wrath (passion, rage, bad temper) and resentment (anger, animosity) and quarreling (brawling, clamor, contention) and slander (evilspeaking, abusive or blasphemous language) be banished from you, with all malice (spite, ill will, or baseness of any kind)."

Jesus also came down hard on bitterness: "Anyone who is angry with his brother will be subject to judgment. . . . Anyone who says, 'You fool!' will be in danger of the fire of hell" (Matt. 5:22). That verse broke my heart once in regard to the bitterness I held against a woman I had reached out to and who had then gone on to take advantage of me. I realized that my bitterness was essentially rebellion against God. I'd broken fellowship with him as well as with her. I had no inner peace until I tracked down her out-of-state address and wrote a difficult letter asking her forgiveness.

The Cross Neutralizes Bitterness

When Moses cried out to God on behalf of his people, God showed him a piece of wood that would solve their problem. But notice that Moses didn't just stretch a branch over the water as he'd stretched his hands over the Red Sea. He had to throw the piece of wood into the water. The solution had to invade the bitterness. That is how Christ works with us. We cannot, by ourselves, solve problems of bitterness. We may be able to cover them up, but we cannot eradicate them.

When we ask Christ to invade our bitterness, he can bring healing, but we must agree to do the things he asks, even if they are hard. Skip Gray of the Navigators ministry speaks of it this way: "If you want to follow Jesus, then you must take up your cross daily, and taking up your cross means forgiving and believing that what someone else meant for your harm, God intended for your good. By so doing you will, amazingly and mysteriously, redeem both the act and the person who did it. You redeem the act by setting him free from his debt to you."[7]

No one said it would be easy. That's why the writer to the Hebrews admonished, *"Make every effort* to live in peace with all men and to be holy; without holiness no one will see the Lord"* (Heb. 12:14; emphasis mine). In verse 15 he supplements that warning with a picture: "See to it that no one misses the grace of God and that no bitter root grows up to cause trouble and defile many." Those of us who do weed duty in our lawns or gardens know how stubborn and deep some roots go. (I especially detest morning glory among my rose bushes. It's impossible!) In the same way, bitterness is a weed whose roots spread like tentacles into places we never imagined.

When we "make every effort" to live peaceably, we agree to face others as honestly as we face God. We go to them with him at our side, stripped of pride and seeking peace with them to match peace with him.

Whenever we get bitter and upset about a difficult situation, we need to end up on our knees, bringing the whole matter to the cross of Jesus Christ. There, the Son of God hung naked while he died in the most excruciating way possible, yet he gasped words of forgiveness. Anyone else would have screamed and raged in bitterness. That's exactly what one of the men crucified beside him did. But not the Son of God.

The change in Lynn's life came with the Easter season. Lynn had wrestled for weeks with the conviction that she needed to go back to the people who had hurt her. On Good Friday, as she headed home from shopping, she sensed the Lord speaking to her: *Lynn, I died to forgive you. The least you can do is forgive them. Today is the ideal day to do that.*

Turning down the street to the church, she silently wished that the minister wouldn't be there or that he would refuse to see her. Instead, his secretary told Lynn to walk right in. Standing in front of his immense wooden desk, Lynn summoned the courage to speak.

"I've come because I feel we need to make peace," she said. "There isn't anybody in town I couldn't walk up and talk to, except you. I don't know what I've done, but I ask your forgiveness. I want to be welcome in this church. I've been deeply hurt. It's taken me a long time. But I need your forgiveness."

Lynn noticed tears flowing down the minister's cheeks as he responded, "I'm so glad you came, because I've wanted to come to you. I didn't know how." Coming around the desk, he hugged her.

"I drove from that church in tears, drained," Lynn says, "but I knew I had done what was right before God. I'd faced the man who hurt me, forgiven him, and asked for his forgiveness. Although there would be coolness between us, we could talk again." Lynn admits that her hurt and anger occasionally try to resurface, "but now I can deal with it as God's finished business."

Leading Us to Sweeter Waters

The bitter waters in Lynn's life were sweetened. But her story didn't end there, no more than the Hebrews' lesson ended at Marah. After that, "they came to Elim, where there were twelve springs and seventy palm trees, and they camped there near the water" (Ex. 15:27). At Marah, God showed how he can sweeten life's bitterness; Elim showed God's grace in providing refreshment along the way. There were individual springs for each of the twelve tribes, and palm trees were sufficient to provide ample shade from the desert heat. God knew his people needed rest and relaxation, and he arranged it.

As Lynn looks back on her "Marah"—that Good Friday when she sought forgiveness—she sees how God also led her to a place of refreshment and hope. She decided to open her own preschool, but had to put aside plans after shoulder surgery. She continued to wrestle with doubts that she could ever teach again. Then one November day, nearly a year after her dismissal, she noticed an ad for a preschool teacher in a large, private day-care center.

She was hired. Half a year later, the director took Lynn out to lunch and told her she wanted to retire and sell the school to Lynn. Lynn first thought she couldn't afford it. Then a few weeks later, she received an inheritance that provided the down payment. By the next fall, she was the new owner and director of a school serving one hundred children, ages two through five.

She opened her first staff meeting by telling workers the school would be operated according to Colossians 3:23-24: "Whatever you do, work at it with all your heart, as working for the Lord, not for men, since you know that you will receive an inheritance from the Lord as a reward. It is the Lord Christ you are serving." To express that, Lynn delivered each employee's paycheck with a hug and a reminder of how much she appreciated them.

Lynn led the school for six years before a stroke slowed her down. But those challenging, invigorating years put a sweet ending on her teaching career. We will never know the whole story behind Lynn's firing. But Lynn applied the cross to her bitterness and went on, healed and ready to make a difference for Christ.

Mileposts

1. Imagine yourself as one of the Hebrews of the Exodus. What things would you need water for? How much water would you take and how would you store it? What would you do when you ran out of water? Look at what your answers reveal about your concept of God's provision. What picture does Psalm 84:5-7 give of a caring God? (Note that "Valley of Baca" means "Valley of Weeping.")
2. After crossing the Red Sea, the Hebrews faced a trackless

desert. There's a parallel here to our own moral wilderness. The Hebrews were guided by God's pillars of cloud and fire (which, by the way, helped provide some protection from the scorching sun and provided warmth for the bone-chilling nights). What do Christians have for guidance? See John 8:12 and 14:6.

3. Has there been an authority figure in your past—such as a boss, teacher, or parent—whom you tended to scorn? Do you harbor bitterness toward that person? Think of times in your life when you've been hurt. As you remember them, do any still upset you? That's a clue that you are still bitter about them. How valid are they in the perspective of Ephesians 4:31-32?

4. Have you ever wished you hadn't said something? Perhaps it was something hurtful or thoughtless. Read James 3:9-12 and think about how it relates to the Marah experience. What's the solution? Read through the rest of James 3 for suggestions.

5. As you write out this chapter's memory verse, draw by it a picture of a weed to help you remember the difficulty of rooting out bitterness: "See to it that no one misses the grace of God and that no bitter root grows up to cause trouble and defile many" (Heb. 12:15).

One does not live by bread alone,
but by every word that comes from the mouth of the LORD.
—*Deuteronomy 8:3*, NRSV

5
You Expect Me to Eat That?

Ingratitude and Thankfulness

We live one golden mile from the Golden Arches and other drive-through sanctuaries of high-fat, high-salt, quickie standardized menus. The first words my first-born muttered after "Mama" and "Dada" were "French fries." By the time a sister arrived, he'd already equated happiness with a burger-bag toy.

I grew up when "Leave It to Beaver" set the standard for family dinners. When I finally married at thirty-four, I presumed my husband and offspring would rim a linen-topped table and speak in hushed tones about my meat loaf. They'd glory in discovering delicacies like Brussels sprouts and pickled beets. And should there ever be a time when I served leftovers, they would exclaim, "How blessed we are to enjoy this feast again."

But I'm afraid my children have changed the basic food groups to cola, cookies, chips, and candy. One of them will eat semi-poisonous foods—green beans, for example—if such food has a generous prelude and postlude of saltine crackers.

I tell them they'll grow up and marry somebody addicted

to tofu and alfalfa sprouts, and that love will change their ways. They remind me of my own failures in the food department. The culinary compulsories of my childhood included oatmeal mush every weekday morning and liver once a month. Both were impossibilities to my palate without being decorated with ample supplies of chocolate chips. To this day, whenever I see cooked oatmeal, I see brown swirls. And when I see liver in the butcher case, I see it cold at 7 P.M., glaring at the stubborn six year old who was forbidden to leave the table until three more bites (crowned with chocolate chips) went down the hatch. When I prayed "Give us this day our daily bread," I was certain that didn't include liver.

When we look to God for what we need for each day, our response to his provision tells much about our spiritual character. Sometimes we get mush or liver and our "gratitude attitude" drops pretty low. We behave like the Hebrews when they ran out of food six weeks after leaving Egypt. "If only we had died by the Lord's hand in Egypt!" they complained. "There we sat around pots of meat and ate all the food we wanted, but you have brought us out into this desert to starve this entire assembly to death" (Ex. 16:3).

God had a solution for this, but it was not what they expected. Their reaction teaches us a lot about their own spiritual condition—and sheds some light on principles that still ring true today:

- We naturally crave things that are not good for us.
- God provides what we need—and just enough of it.
- God's nourishment is perfect.
- Spiritual food comes in individual portions.

Craving What We Shouldn't

The Hebrews wanted Egypt's food again, but they forgot that it came with an unsavory sauce called slavery. Numbers 11:5 says they even daydreamed over Egypt's cucumbers, melons, leeks, onions, and garlic!

I can't imagine anything more disgusting. One time my husband and I tried a diet whose anchor is a soup made of onions, cabbage, celery, green bell peppers, and tomatoes. It came from the kitchen of a hospital that specializes in heart surgeries, and it is designed for overweight folks who need to quickly drop ten pounds. The instructions say you can eat all the soup you want. The more you eat, the more you lose. After three days of this wretched soup, we wondered why any sane person would *want* to eat it! Maybe that's the secret of the diet.

Any dieter will affirm that we crave what's not good for us. We do this in life, too. I've cried with too many women friends who craved marriage and family but went for cheap substitutes, then found themselves unwed mothers. Or, they married somebody who wasn't a Christian because they couldn't wait for God's best—and they now regret it.

So often what we think we want isn't God's best. Sometimes even innocent aspirations, like doing well in business, can pull us away from God.

Doug and Shirley Hunter would agree. From the start of their marriage, Shirley and Doug seemed to have everything going for them. Both were Christians. They'd begun successful careers: Shirley as a teacher and Doug as a social worker at a boys' rehabilitation ranch. But they soon learned that a bacterial infection—possibly from a siege of flu—had damaged Doug's aortic valve. Five months after their wedding, surgeons implanted a pig's valve in Doug's weak heart. Yet as Doug recovered from that surgery, a bigger "heart" problem became evident.

"Our marriage was a struggle," Doug admits. "Shirley and I had read extensively about marriage, and I was doing marriage counseling at work. But at home we fought like cats and dogs. Shirley didn't want the sun going down on our anger, but I wouldn't cooperate. My boss was also our pastor. I couldn't tell him our marriage was hurting. Only the pressure of hiding our problems kept us together."

Then came another devastating event. They were involved

in a prosperous business that required a lot of travel. One April day in 1978 they faced a long trip home. By evening, Doug was beat, so Shirley offered to take the wheel for a while. It was close to midnight as she set the cruise control on their new Porsche. Doug quickly dozed off. Within half an hour, so did Shirley.

Shirley woke just in time to see their car racing toward a cement divider. She jerked the steering wheel and the car rolled, crushing the driver's side. When it came to rest, Doug looked over and thought Shirley was dead.

"Dear God!" he cried. "Please don't let her die! Please bring her back to me!"

Lying on her stomach, her body twisted, Shirley roused enough to tell Doug she was okay. She added, "Honey, could you move whatever's on my legs so I can move them?"

Doug's heart sank. There was nothing on her legs. He held her bleeding head as paramedics poked her skin with needles. From the neck down, she felt nothing. Emergency room X-rays revealed that Shirley's spine was severed between the sixth and seventh vertebrae. Paralysis of her hands and legs was certain. Doug was devastated.

Both Doug and Shirley had grown up in homes where their parents had taught them about God's love. Following his own heart surgery, Doug had learned that God could carry him through hard times. But he couldn't help wondering what God could bring out of this.

God Provides What We Need

God made an object lesson of his ability to provide when the Hebrews ran out of food. God dispatched a wind to nudge a flock of migrating quail right into the Hebrews' campsite. Kentucky Fried—just for the grabbing! But even the Colonel's recipe tastes better with biscuits, and so the next morning God sent something so unique and unnameable that its name literally means "What is it?" "I will rain down bread from heaven for you. The people are to go out each day and gather enough for that day" (Ex. 16:4). And so they began forty years of manna in the morning, manna in the noontime, manna at suppertime.

Manna was as mysterious to the Hebrews as moon rocks are to us. Exodus 16:31 says it was "white like coriander seed and tasted like wafers made with honey." Some theorize it was the excretion of the two types of local insects or a type of lichen that grows on rocks. But that doesn't explain how this nutritionally complete substance fell in enough abundance to feed some two million people.

It fell six mornings of the week for each day's meals. On the sixth day, twice as much fell so they wouldn't have to gather food on the Sabbath. Except for the Sabbath food, anything they tried to hoard overnight got foul and wormy.

God has used this passage to speak to me about hoarding and wanting more and more. One of the richest men in the world was asked how much money would make him happy. His reply: "Just a little more." I wrestle with that "little more," for example, in regard to our economy-size "starter home." When I visit friends with bigger houses (and bigger mortgages!) I sometimes mentally move in. I also think of how, someday, we might need to enfold my widowed mother-in-law into our living space. Then God asks me how much "more" I need. We sponsor two children through compassion ministries—one in Haiti and the other in Zaire. Both have lost a parent; we presume the African child's father, a pastor, was murdered in the civil war. Are we not abundantly blessed in comparison to these children?

Our affluent culture raises our expectations for contentment. Seasonal style changes encourage us to get bored with our clothes—yet Deuteronomy 8:4 says the Hebrews' clothes didn't wear out for forty years. Then there's the lure of cars. I especially remember one television ad for a luxury car. The ad promoted the typical vicarious experience of driving a powerful vehicle over velvet roads in purple-mountain-majesty surroundings. But I smiled over the irony of the ad's music, the soothing folk hymn "'Tis a Gift to Be Simple." To match that song, they should have advertised a faithful, bruised clunker!

Don Baker relates another picture of needs versus wants in his little book *The Way of the Shepherd*. In talking about contented sheep—their bellies full, their spirits at rest beside quiet waters—he recalled memories of his grandmother. Widowed, diabetic, and poor, she lived in a drafty, one-bedroom house across from her church. She had a wood stove, an old oil heater, and no carpet on the floor. She walked two blocks to cash her welfare check and had her groceries delivered. Her parents, husband, and two of her twelve children were dead; the rest had moved away. "But I never heard her complain," he wrote. "She was content. Whenever I'd ask if I could get her anything, the answer was always the same, 'I have everything I need.' In this greedy grasping world of ours, that sort of contentment is rare."[8]

Doug and Shirley's accident jolted them into reassessing their standards for contentment. As Shirley lay helpless in the hospital, Doug cried for three days, humbled over nearly losing his wife, and releasing his bitterness over their marital problems. "Instead of fighting God, I accepted that he loved me and that he was in control," Doug said. "Instead of running from God, I ran to him, and he gave me a new love for Shirley."

That first month, manna began sprinkling into Doug's life as he stayed with Christian friends in Seattle, who lived near the hospital where Shirley was sent for rehabilitation.

"The wife knew I wanted to be at the hospital by 8:00 A.M.," Doug recalled. "She'd get up early to pray and study her Bible. When I came down for breakfast, she'd say, 'Doug, let me tell you what I studied this morning.' She'd talk for about a minute, then pray for breakfast. I soaked it in like a dry sponge. Every morning I'd think about her little devotional pearls as I rode my bike the 3.5 miles to see Shirley." By the time Doug reached her hospital room, Shirley recalls, "he was just glowing."

Health specialists warned them that ninety percent of

marriages involving quadriplegia end in divorce. Doug and Shirley became part of the ten percent who not only coped, but thrived. Doug got hospital permission to improvise a double bed in Shirley's room so he could stay round-the-clock with her. They lived off their savings as he personally contributed as much as he could toward her care and rehabilitation.

Eight months after the accident, Shirley came home, re-learning to keep house with mobility in only her upper arms. At first, even simple tasks overwhelmed her. Pulling on pants took thirty minutes, since she could only use her palms. Her first attempt at baking cookies took two days. Doug helped as he could, but he also had to concentrate on his new job as a fruit broker.

But just as he watched over the Israelites in the desert, God saw Shirley's very real physical needs. Her retired parents moved 350 miles north, buying a home just five blocks from Shirley and Doug's. Her mother began what became years of daily trips to help Shirley with housework and personal hygiene. She also became Shirley's chauffeur and cheer-leader as Shirley began to speak and sing at women's meetings and nursing homes.

God also saw Doug and Shirley's needs to relax together. "We learned to thank God for those leisure activities we could still enjoy rather than focusing on what was no longer possible," Shirley says. "Doug wanted me to continue to enjoy all that life offered. With adjustments for my paralysis, we even went rafting, snowmobiling, and horseback riding. We celebrated one anniversary with a glider ride."

Doug and Shirley got more involved in their new church, hosting a marriage enrichment class in their home and sharing their faith at churches and couples' retreats. They became a part of the Gideons' Bible distribution program. Doug was so committed to sharing God's Word with others that he even took a suitcase of Spanish Bibles along on their vacation trips to Mexico. In Cabo San Lucas, on the tip of the Baja Peninsula, there's now a church begun by believers who became Christians through Doug's witness.

Perfect Nutrition

Manna was all the food groups in one compact form. The Hebrews didn't need vitamin supplements! But they didn't appreciate God's provision, nor could they comprehend how their daily food-fall held extraordinary symbolism for spiritual contentment.

> He humbled you by letting you go hungry and then feeding you with manna, a food previously unknown to you and your ancestors. He did it to teach you that people need more than bread for their life; real life comes by feeding on every word of the LORD. (Deuteronomy 8:3, NLT)

Manna represents Jesus Christ, who in John 6 called himself the Bread of Life. He also called himself the Word, for all that he did helped explain the Father. As we read and apply God's Word, taking in knowledge of him and his commands for living, we are rebuilt spiritually, just as real food rebuilds the millions of cells within our physical bodies. As we feast on Jesus, his humility, perfection, and purity will become a part of us. That's why Paul could write, "Godliness with contentment is great gain" (1 Tim. 6:6) and "I have learned the secret of being content in any and every situation" (Phil. 4:12). Contentment comes from finding both God's provision and his Person sufficient.

Doug and Shirley learned that lesson as physical challenges continued to flood their lives. By the end of 1986, Doug had undergone three more open-heart surgeries. In the last, eleven-hour surgery, Doug nearly died as surgeons struggled to patch seventy percent of an aorta destroyed by a staph infection. Then in 1990, while driving to church, Doug blacked out. With a desperate prayer, Shirley reached an arm over the wheel and pulled the car to safety. Doug was rushed to the hospital, where his heart stopped in the emergency room. Within minutes, doctors installed a pacemaker to save him.

A month later, on her fortieth birthday, Shirley learned she had breast cancer; she subsequently went through a lumpectomy, radiation treatments, and chemotherapy. The same day, Doug was diagnosed with congestive heart failure, a condition to be later complicated by another staph infection.

In November 1994, Doug learned he had lymphoma and began chemotherapy. Half a year later, doctors found another lump in Shirley's breast, and two days later Doug's CAT scan revealed that his cancer had returned. Shirley underwent a mastectomy while Doug pursued lymphoma treatments, including a special immune-boosting/cleansing therapy in Mexico. Hundreds across the nation prayed for them. But Doug's body couldn't rally, and he died fourteen months after the disease was diagnosed.

After his death, Shirley became aware of a pressing pain in her chest, which she felt was more than the heaviness of grief. Doctors traced the pain to a problem related to her spinal cord injury. At the same time, they found a lump under her left arm, which revealed another breast cancer. A second mastectomy followed.

People who didn't know Shirley well wondered how she coped. When I put that question to her, I knew part of the answer was "manna," her lifelong intake of God's Word and communion with him. "My parents gave me a wonderful foundation," she recalled. "Every day we had family devotions. Mom or Dad would read the Bible, one of us kids would read from a little devotional magazine, and then we'd pray. It made a huge impression on my heart about God's love and call on my life." After the accident, every night Shirley and Doug read the Bible, talked about it, and prayed together. Having that common spiritual basis made it easier to go to God in prayer and search Scripture for direction and comfort.

"When the trials got harder," Shirley recalls, "we'd always go to the Psalms. When Doug was his sickest during therapy in Mexico, he had me read Psalms continually to him. David and the other writers praised God even when things looked impossible, and that spoke to the deepest parts of our spirits."

Shirley also found herself sustained by spiritual manna in cards and letters sent by Christian friends. Many shared Bible verses of compassion and hope. One friend, for example, wrote of how she changed from griping about life's daily irritants to using those times as reminders to pray for Shirley.

"Corrie ten Boom told a story of how her father said God would give us the ticket at just the right time," Shirley says. "I know God inspired those people to write what they did at just the right time to minister to me. I cried when I read them and I cry when I re-read them. But they're like God's drops of love and mercy, reminders of his care expressed through the many people I know."

Collecting Spiritual Manna One Portion at a Time

Each Hebrew gathered about three pints of manna off the ground every day. It was hard work plucking little scale-like globs off the desert sand! (We have blueberry bushes, and I know how long it takes to pick a couple of pints of berries.) But again, God had a purpose. He wanted them to realize their utter dependence on him. He wanted them to come to him for a fresh supply every day.

In the same way, we need a fresh supply of God's Word daily. Some people argue, "Well, I read through the Bible in 1966 (or 1982 or 1995). I know all there is to know." That's like leftovers discovered in the church refrigerator—the ones where the cleanup crew snickers, "You see this container labeled 'Watson'? They left the church five years ago!" Old manna turns stale. We need the fresh stuff! And I know every time I read through the Bible, I find new treasures.

Notice, too, that the Israelites gathered manna every

morning before the sun melted it. Of course, no Bible verse declares, "Thou must have devotions in the morning." But there's something special about the morning shift, starting the day settled with the mind of God.

We also should pick up the morsels ourselves. Yes, we need teaching from pastors, Bible study leaders, and other Christian teachers. God appoints pastors and teachers to help build us up spiritually (Eph. 4:11-12). But there's nothing like being alone with God, reading his Word, and asking, "How should this apply to my life? What does this say about my faith, my relationship problems, my secret sins?" That's when Scripture really gets inside and changes us.

We also need to make sure we're picking up *God's* manna. Human philosophies might motivate us for a time, but they won't answer the deepest questions of life nor supernaturally enable us to survive life's tough times. When I was raising support for mission service, I was invited to speak to a women's Bible study. When the lady assigned to do devotions got up and said, "I have just discovered the prophet," I expected some morsels from Jeremiah or Isaiah. To my shock, she quoted from *The Prophet* by Syrian-born poet Kahlil Gibran! It was quite an act to follow, telling how the mission group I was joining wanted to get God's Word into yet unwritten languages, because only Jesus can change lives.

It's hard to explain how God's Word changes us, yet we know when it happens. The inner transformation can also affect our demeanor. You can't miss, for example, the hope in Shirley's eyes and the gentle vibrancy in her conversation. She has a composure despite tragedy that can only come from God. I was reminded of that the day of Doug's funeral. From the balcony of a packed church, I watched as Doug's coffin was rolled in and Shirley followed in her wheelchair. She wore white—her visual statement that Doug's death meant the pure hope of resurrection. And while the rest of us bit back tears, recalling the impact of their lives and how difficulties pressed them closer to God and each other, Shirley sang. In her strong, warm alto voice, she who could not walk sang the chorus, "Precious Lord, take my hand, lead me on, help me stand." As she sang, every phrase affirmed her conviction that God would still walk beside her.

Even so, Shirley will admit life isn't always easy.

"I really struggled after Doug died," she says. "We'd taken good care of our bodies. We ate healthy foods—lots of vegetables, fruits, chicken, and fish. We don't drink or smoke. Yet we got cancer. And, in spite of all we did and all the prayers, Doug died. About half a year after his death, I was really feeling dry and empty. One Sunday our pastor preached on the parable of the lost coin. He urged us to identify something we'd lost in our lives that we needed to find again. As I prayed afterward with friends, I saw I'd lost my trust and absolute faith in God."

Shirley felt this loss highlighted when she began to write a friend who was waiting for a heart transplant. She wanted to encourage him to believe God would restore him. "But when I tried to write," Shirley says, "I sensed a blockage in really believing what I knew I should say. Since I couldn't get down on my real knees to pray, I had to get down on mental knees and tell the Lord I wanted to get back to the way I used to feel about him. I yearned to encourage my friend with a transparent heart."

The following Sunday, though struggling with physical pain and emotional reluctance, Shirley felt a spiritual release during the church service and couldn't stop crying.

"As we gathered in prayer groups, I realized God's love was washing away the doubts and mistrust in my heart," she says. "I could affirm that God had everything under control. Even though there were still big questions, I could accept that I wouldn't understand it all until I got to heaven. And I could be satisfied with God alone."

Shirley's response reminds me of a scene in *The Boyhood of Ranald Bannerman* by nineteenth-century Scottish novelist George MacDonald. Ranald's father, a pastor, had taken the boy along to visit John, a godly church member who was dying.

"Well, John," the pastor said, "you've had a hard life of it."

"No harder than I could bear," said John.

"It's a grand thing to be able to say that," said Ranald's father.

"Oh sir, for that matter, I would go through it all again, if it was his will, and willingly. I have no will but his, sir."[9]

How do we come to that point? I believe through a steady walk with God, nurtured by the manna of God's Word and the knowledge that God knows what we need. "You have made known to me the path of life," says Psalm 16:11. "You will fill me with joy in your presence, with eternal pleasures at your right hand." We can have that lasting, deep satisfaction when we feed with grateful hearts upon the Bread of Life.

Early one November, when my daughter Inga was eleven, she decided we needed something more to our Thanksgiving celebration than turkey, football, and the traditional centerpiece of Grandma's pilgrim candles nestled in fall leaves. So I helped her cover a basket with fabric and cut a slit in the top for "thankful notes." All that month our family stuffed it with notes about what we were thankful for. On Thanksgiving night, we opened the basket and read each others' notes.

Our thanks went for things like the car getting fixed after Mom was rear-ended. For good books. Good grades. Fairly good health. Braces (and orthodontic payment!). Each other. Hugs. Salvation.

Our lives aren't perfect. We juggle debts, loved ones dying, tough situations at work, house repairs, overloaded schedules, and other challenges that are a part of living. But we have so much to be thankful for—most of all, God's Word, his love, and his promise of eternal life.

Mileposts

1. What are the "if only's" in your life—the things you tend to complain about? Be honest! Evaluate those things against Philippians 2:14-16.

2. The manna incident took place in the southwest Sinai Peninsula, in a place called the "Wilderness of Sin." The place name has no connection to our English word *sin*, but what sins were evident there? Read Exodus 16 and look for the verbs that reveal attitude problems.

3. Manna is called a "type" or symbol of Christ because it illustrates him and his ministry. Read John 6:25-59 and list the ways Christ compares with the Israelite manna.

4. How are you taking in spiritual manna? What changes do you need to make in your spiritual life? Make a bookmark and write on it Deuteronomy 8:3: "One does not live by bread alone, but by every word that comes from the mouth of the LORD" (NRSV). If you've never read through the Bible, start today. If you have, start again.

5. For memory, tuck away this reminder of Christ, our Manna: "I am the bread of life. Whoever comes to me will never be hungry, and whoever believes in me will never be thirsty" (John 6:35, NRSV).

Tremble, O earth, at the presence of the Lord, . . .
who turned the rock into a pool,
the hard rock into springs of water.—Psalm 114:7-8

6
When the Water Bottles Run Out . . .

Discouragement and Trust

There's nothing like substituting on a 115-customer paper route to teach children the realities of life. At least, that's what I told myself as I sat panting in a sizzling black car with two quickly vaporizing preteens one triple-digit summer afternoon, waiting for the paper truck drop-off.

I was their "wheels" to the route site and, consequently, the senior boss of the delivery committee. If I helped, we'd get home faster to the healing breezes of our air conditioner. Besides, they could use my help. This wasn't your normal toss-the-paper-near-the-porch route. Most of it was a senior citizens mobile-home park, laid out like a maze for laboratory rats, and the customers were persnickety about where their papers should go. Any mistake would mar the record of the regular delivery person, who just happened to be the wife of my children's principal. (She'd kept her son's old route after he left for college.) And if there's anybody you want to impress when you're twelve and fourteen, it's your principal and other ominous adults.

The things a mother will do to teach her children responsibility and character (and maintain her own reputation)!

"I'm dying," my daughter moaned, as she flung her legs out an open car door providing the nearest shade. The other child didn't talk; he was too busy pouring water down his throat. After a half hour of charbroiling next to the drop-off point, I knocked on a friendly door to borrow a phone. The press had broken down, I was told. We'd have to wait a little longer. I drove the kids home to refill their water bottles, then returned to resume our vigil. "The truck should be here any minute, and then we'll deliver those papers in a wink," I said.

Perhaps I was lying. But how else could I motivate two pooped-out pubescents to run papers in sizzling temperatures for the next hour and a quarter?

I reminded them that I could bail out. Then they wouldn't have Dear Old Mom pulling the little red wagon stacked with newsprint and telling them what to do ("1310 Icicle, front porch in a plastic bag, tip it up so the lady doesn't have to bend over"). At least we had our water bottles. By the end of the route, they were empty.

Thirst is a powerful human craving. It's also a powerful spiritual symbol, highlighted in Exodus 17 when the Hebrews drank the last of the water they'd brought from Elim. The incident explores two opposite traits—discouragement and trust—with these lessons:

- God wants to expand our view of his sufficiency.
- God honors our obedience.
- Our testimonies are continually on display.
- Nothing can separate us from God's love.

God's Great Sufficiency

One morning as I went shopping with my daughter, then age thirteen, she started talking about what career she'd follow when she grew up. We quickly eliminated newspaper delivery person, Olympic ice skater, and math professor! As she mulled other job possibilities, my first thought was that she needed to make good wages, because she loves to shop!

As much as I might like to choose a stable career and a worry-free life for her, I realize that the lean and discouraging times are important parts of our spiritual journeys—for our children and for all of us.

My husband is a rare "Steady Eddie," who for thirty years has taught elementary physical education to hundreds of children. Every month of our marriage, we've had a paycheck. We don't live extravagantly (Rich's major weakness is garage sales; mine is fabric stores), but we've been able to pay our bills and put some away in savings. We both remember leaner times as singles. While he taught and paid off college debts, I bounced all over the map with short-term mission service, fill-in-the-gap jobs, and graduate work. Though I lived frugally, I really had to look to God to stretch what I had or bring in unexpected income. Sometimes a one-day typing job went straight for groceries. But I always had something to eat and a place to live.

It was hard to have God test my trust. But I clung to the certainty that he was watching over me: "I was young and now I am old, yet I have never seen the righteous forsaken or their children begging bread" (Ps. 37:25). I wouldn't have to beg bread. I wouldn't even have to stand on a corner and play my violin with the case open on the sidewalk.

But the thirsty Hebrews lacked that conviction as they camped at Rephidim. Instead of trusting, they grumbled. "Why," they accused Moses, "did you bring us up out of Egypt to make us and our children and livestock die of thirst?" (Ex. 17:3). They were so upset, they were ready to stone Moses. At Marah and Elim they had water, though one source was foul. Here, there was nothing—just desert. What a great opportunity for God to exhibit his omnipotence!

Trusting God in the midst of discouragement is a hard lesson—one that some learn better than others. I learned about it in watching the lives of John and Nancy Meacham. We met after my cousin Sandy (their friend) alerted me that they were moving to my town. I found John and Nancy to be courageous, devout people who lived out God's Word as they parented their seven children. One time we had them over for dinner. I'd never fed such a big family before and so I settled on turkey soup. Somehow, we all squeezed into my ten-by-sixteen kitchen/dining room. I was amazed by the extraordinarily good manners of the children—even the baby! John and Nancy were doing the parenting "thing" right.

I learned how their faith was rooted in the conviction that God had created them for glorifying him. Nancy was adopted, and she was the first Christian in her adoptive family, followed by her parents, a brother, and several in-laws. At college she met John, an ROTC officer and—most importantly—a Christian.

As newlyweds they moved to Pennsylvania, where John studied communications and Nancy taught in an urban school. After reading David Wilkerson's book *The Cross and the Switch-blade,* she realized God could work even greater things in their lives. Immediately she tested the Lord, asking him to cause a certain incorrigible student to do his homework.

"It was inconceivable," she remembers. "He never handed in any assignments. But the next morning when I entered the classroom, I saw this boy beaming, holding out his homework! Clearly, God was interested in my prayers and wanted me to have a closer relationship with him."

During John's Air Force training in Alabama, the couple experienced what it meant to have Jesus as their source of Living Water and surrendered their lives to him for service. They learned to live securely "on the edge," knowing God had the resources and power to care for and protect them.

God Honors Our Obedience

At Rephidim, God gave the Israelites an object lesson of his care: he told Moses to whack a certain rock with the same staff that had divided the Red Sea. I love to imagine the scene as water gushed out. Delirious with joy, men and women surged toward it, splashing it on their faces, cupping it to their mouths, savoring the freshness pouring down their throats, scooping it in pots, and letting it flow past their sand-calloused feet.

Some scholars contend that Moses just cracked a weak shale plug off an underground stream. But how could he know where to hit—unless God showed him? And how do we explain the abundance of water—enough to quench the thirst of two million people and their livestock? Only God, who created that landscape, could have caused a flow that exceeded all natural laws.

But Rephidim was more than a mammoth watering trough. It's a picture of Jesus Christ, who described himself as the Living Water, the One who could quench every spiritual thirst: "If you are thirsty, come to me! If you believe in me, come and drink! For the Scriptures declare that rivers of living water will flow out from within" (John 7:37-38, NLT). We're so prone to drag along in our Christian lives, discouraged by every crisis that comes our way. That's not what God intends. He wants us to stay by him, close to his Son the Rock, drinking up the spiritual refreshment that keeps us living steady for the Lord.

When John and Nancy's tight finances got even tighter, John looked at the crisis as an opportunity to follow God to another place. They moved to Fort Indiantown Gap, Pennsylvania, where John became commander of the Air National Guard's 211th Engineer Installation Squadron. After moving nineteen times in their twenty-one years of marriage, Nancy was grateful for the roots they were beginning to put down in Pennsylvania.

It was their habit to walk together after dinner, to talk and plan. Nancy's days spun around the needs of their children, while John carried a heavy load with the Guard. One particular night, Nancy soaked in the colors of late fall and the peaceful landscape of their rural neighborhood. Nothing could have prepared her for what John revealed as they ended their walk.

"Nancy," he said, as they paused in the driveway, "God told me I have less than two years to live."

Nancy's mind whirled. She could think of seven reasons, ages three to eighteen, for John to live. No, there were eight reasons. Nancy needed him, too. But she had watched John walk closely with God, and she knew he'd learned not to dismiss the still, small voice of his Lord. One time, for example, he felt God impressing them to give an odd amount of money to a couple expecting their third baby. They later learned that their gift, plus the couple's savings, covered their hospital bill to the penny. "I was grateful for a godly husband," Nancy recalls. "But I found this premonition of death hard to accept."

John was so certain of God's message that he even wrote out final instructions for his family and coworkers. He also wrote personal letters to Nancy and to each child, to be opened after his death. "Though it seemed John was dwelling on the prospect of death, his concern for these details made me feel secure," Nancy said.

Testimonies on Display

Exodus 17:6 says Moses struck the rock in the sight of the elders of Israel. God wanted a host of official witnesses to see that he really loved his people and had a plan for them. It's a reminder that none of us is on earth by accident. God has a grand plan.

Psychologists and social scientists have noted that every human being seeks to fulfill needs that range from basic survival to a sense of self-worth. The Hebrews were struggling with their most basic need—survival. They needed water for themselves and their livestock. Beyond that, they needed a sense of belonging, of tribal connectedness as Hebrews and as the children of God. One purpose of the Exodus was to mold a disjointed group of former slaves into a nation. After that would come fulfillment, the sense that they were indeed God's chosen people and they would settle in a land they could call their own.

Finally, they would seek God's approval and the sense of a destiny bigger than themselves. They clung to prophecies that said their bloodlines would produce the Messiah.

Those needs come down to each of us. From the moment of birth, when cold air shocks our little lungs, we cry out for those things necessary for survival. Through families we seek to belong with others. In training for a life occupation and purpose, we seek something that fulfills our abilities and interests. That connectedness and self-fulfillment combine best in what is called the servant life. E. Stanley Jones explains it in *The Unshakable Kingdom:*

> The most miserable people in the world are the people who are self-centered, who don't do anything for anybody, except themselves. On the contrary, the happiest people are the people who deliberately take on themselves the sorrows and troubles of others. Their hearts sing with a strange, wild joy, automatically and with no exceptions. We are structured for the outgoingness of the love of the kingdom. It is our native land.[10]

When we look down the road and see a cemetery, we're reminded that life is nothing unless we seek something bigger than ourselves, something that will take our efforts and declare them "good" forever. Jesus knows all about these longings. He offers the "abundant life" (John 10:10), the one that can meet every person's need. Because of his death and resurrection, we can gain a spiritual re-energizing through his Holy Spirit. As we drink of him, we can find strength we never knew possible for life's tough times.

On November 7, 1992, two years after the evening walk in which John told Nancy of his premonition of dying, John finished up his Saturday yard work and told Nancy he was going over to the neighbor's house. Nancy, busy fixing dinner, guessed at the reason for his visit. The neighbor's thirty-six-year-old son, who lived at home, had a history of drug abuse and an obsession with guns.

Many times the Meachams had experienced his temper and persecution complex. Recently, the son had been shooting at groundhogs in his backyard, and John and Nancy were understandably concerned for their children's safety. The son also had complained irrationally about an electric line the Meachams had installed.

As Nancy mopped the kitchen floor, an uneasiness crept over her. John was taking too long. Then another neighbor came to the door. "Nancy," he said, "I think you ought to know there's been a double fatality next door." Nancy began shaking. "John's there," she cried.

The neighbor quickly left to check. When he returned with two policemen, Nancy knew the awful truth. John, only forty-six, was dead. The neighbor's son had come home and found John talking with his parents. He went in his room, got his guns, and shot John in the chest from ten feet away with a .44 Magnum, nicking John's heart. Then he put a 12-gauge shotgun to John's left ear. Finally, as his horrified parents watched, he killed himself.

"My shock in losing John," Nancy says, "was quickly followed by the realization that it happened just as he said it would. And John was ready."

One of John's major concerns had been his family's financial provision. As a large family on a modest income, they'd always lived simply. He took to heart Proverbs 13:22: "A good man leaves an inheritance for his children's children." Another favorite was 1 Timothy 5:8: "If anyone does not provide for his relatives, and especially for his immediate family, he has denied the faith and is worse than an unbeliever." His greatest desire was that his family would have adequate finances if he should die and that Nancy wouldn't have to work outside the home.

"John had prayed that he'd live past June 1992," Nancy recalls. "That gave him twenty years service in the National Guard, entitling me to an annuity."

More God-ordained planning—the water from the rock—came to light. Two days before John died, he bought back a retirement fund that he had cashed out years before when they needed the money. With an inheritance from his grandmother, they then paid off their mortgage—just the day before he was shot. John's funeral expenses were paid through a crime victims' compensation law. Several months after his death, the family received an unexpected lump sum death benefit of $10,000.

But John also left a spiritual inheritance, encapsulated in the letters he had written to Nancy and the children. "We read those letters the day after the shootings," Nancy said. "How grateful I was that he took the time to leave, in his own handwriting, something so precious."

Nancy's letter summarized the financial picture and detailed what personal items to remove from his office. He wanted his wedding ring passed on to one of the children. He named his choice of pallbearers. He wanted Nancy to feel free to remarry, but urged her to delay major decisions for a year. He emphasized his desire that the children be raised to follow Christ and be educated in Christian schools. Letters to the children admonished them to serve and love the Lord with all their hearts.

Nancy felt moved to share these letters beyond the immediate family. So she put the first page of hers on John's casket, where it was seen by many of the 600 people who attended his funeral. John was remembered for his church leadership and his work in establishing a Christian radio station in the area. Many, including the soldiers he commanded, were touched by his testimony. John's witness for Christ was further underscored as copies of Billy Graham's salvation pamphlet, "Steps to Peace with God," were passed out to those at the funeral. Thirty people, including John's brother, decided to follow Christ.

God's Inseparable Love

Our tendency to get discouraged in life's tough times is reflected in the two names given to that water site at Rephidim. *Massah* means "tempting" or "testing"—for here the Israelites tested God. Exodus 17:7 says they had the audacity to suggest God was pulling a mean trick on them, dragging them into the desert and then abandoning them: "Is the Lord among us or not?" The other name, *Meribah* ("chiding" or "strife"), refers to their confrontation with Moses. How often do we complain that God doesn't give us what we want? Or blame others for our problems? Instead, we need to know that God wants to pour hope and help through our lives.

After John's death, Nancy experienced comfort in ways only God could have orchestrated. As the family got ready to go to church the day after his murder, thirteen-year-old Heather quoted Romans 8:28 to her mother: "In all things God works for the good of those who love him." During the ride to church, that same verse came over the car radio. The following Sunday, the soloist's song—chosen at least a month before—was an arrangement of the same verse.

"I sat with tears streaming down my face as she sang," Nancy says. "For the third time, God used that Scripture to affirm his care for me."

About a week after her father's death, Heather dreamed that she and her mother were in the same room with John's body. As they watched his spirit leave his body, he turned and said, "Everything's going to be okay." Then an angel escorted him to heaven. When Heather woke, she had a peace about her father's death.

A week and a half later, Nancy made the lonely walk across the property lines to talk with the parents of her husband's killer. They'd not only lost a son but bore the stigma of his crime. She was touched as the father greeted her with an affirmation of his own faith by saying, "Jesus is my Lord and Savior." As she sat on the very couch where John died, she learned how this father had lost his own father to an accidental shooting. He now feared the Meacham children would have to be farmed out to relatives, as he and his siblings were. "I tried to express our love to them and share our conviction that John's life wasn't cut short in God's perspective," Nancy says. "It was simply his time to die."

Still, Nancy had to deal with the sting of her loss. John's murder had come at a point in their marriage where their relationship had become "especially precious," she says. "Four weeks before, John had begun leading a Bible study on marriage and home life. As we worked on the lessons, we also worked through some of the petty problems of our marriage. When he died, those areas were mended."

Three months later, her first Valentine's Day as a widow loomed. In the past, she and John had attended fund-raising sweetheart banquets for a Christian counseling center. This year she wasn't sure if she wanted to attend alone. Finally, she decided to go as a kitchen helper.

"As I drove to the banquet site, I broke down and cried," Nancy recalls. "Then Hebrews 12:2 suddenly came to mind, about how Jesus endured the cross because of the joy set before him. I realized that John's murder was my cross. Even though the children and I greatly miss him, we'll someday experience real joy when we join him in heaven."

Nancy respected John's request that she wait a year before making any major decisions. But she felt the family needed to move back to the West Coast, nearer relatives and long-time friends. Fifteen months after his death, she and her youngest daughter flew to Vancouver, Washington, where she hoped to live. The trip verified for her how God takes special care of the widow.

"I'd already talked to the Lord about the home I hoped to find," Nancy said. "I told him I wanted something with a wrap-around front porch, two-car attached garage, woods, a stream, and Christian neighbors. My faith wasn't that great— I didn't think the Lord could arrange all that. I told my mother-in-law I didn't think we'd be moving out."

Nancy did know which church she wanted her family to attend, one across the river in Portland. "I asked the Lord to show us through something happening at that church whether we should move there," she says. "I told the Lord I wouldn't manipulate and seek out people. I'd just wait in the lobby with my daughter and see who God would bring to us."

The first person who greeted them was the church's Vancouver-district pastor, who told them about a home for sale by owner next to a church couple's home. Later at church, Nancy met that family and got more information on the house. The next day she made an appointment to see the house.

"As soon as we drove up, I knew it was exactly the house I had asked God for," she said. "Nine Christian neighbors, a wrap-around porch, a stream and woods, two-car attached garage, plus a barn and outbuilding I could use when I started my home business of a reading clinic!"

Now settled in Vancouver, Nancy and her family continue to experience God's care. That trust embraces everything from gas and safety on trips, to choices for life partners. Knowing God was in control helped Nancy relax when one daughter broke an engagement, then met another young man more suited to her personality and gifts, whom she married. Nancy admits she, too, has had several suitors. "But each time, I've been thankful I didn't marry," she says. "I know I can be content serving God single." Nancy has experienced water from the Rock. She will affirm that God can meet your needs at just the right time, even when you're at your lowest and others think God has forgotten you.

Rephidim shows God yearning to pour his abundant refreshment over us. "Come, all you who are thirsty," God said through the prophet Isaiah, "come to the waters; and you who have no money, come, buy and eat!" (Isa. 55:1). Even when we have nothing to offer him but our needs, God stands ready to supply.

Mileposts

1. Name a time when you were most discouraged. Which of these passages comes closest to describing your feelings: Psalm 31:10; Psalm 73:2; Proverbs 13:12?

2. What is the deepest longing of your heart? Companion-ship? Check out John 15:15. Appreciation? Look up Hebrews 6:10. More purpose in life? Read 2 Corinthians 5:17-21. You can't get a bigger purpose than that!

3. First Corinthians 10:3-4 compares Christ to the rock that provided water. What qualities mark the "water" that Christ offers? See John 4:10; Romans 6:23; Ephesians 2:8; and Psalm 105:41.

4. For years the Rock of Gibraltar, a large limestone mass near the entrance of the Mediterranean Sea, has been viewed as a symbol of security and protection. Look up 2 Samuel 22:32, then list ways the spiritual rock named there compares with Gibraltar.

5. Memory verse: "Trust in the Lord with all your heart and lean not on your own understanding; in all your ways acknowledge him, and he will make your paths straight" (Prov. 3:5-6).

Not that we are competent in ourselves to claim anything for ourselves, but our competence comes from God.
—*2 Corinthians 3:5*

7

There Are Monsters under the Bed!

Defeatism and Anticipation

Hey, this must be like driving a car!" my daughter exclaimed as she sat at my sewing machine, going klunkety-klunk in slow motion around the edges of a stuffed-animal project for her home economics/health class. "You put your foot on the pedal and off it goes."

In four years, she'll find out there's more to driving a car, I thought. Two thin pieces of fabric are no comparison to a ton of metal—except when that metal machine starts going *klunkety-klunk, squiddy-soosh, chick-chick, thumpaladunk,* or *whizzy whizzy* underneath. Before I married and my husband took charge of such woes, I'm sure the car repair guys tossed a quick coin to decide who'd get stuck interpreting my descriptions of mechanical misbehavior.

Like the time just after I'd had my snow tires taken off. About a mile down the road, I heard this *CLACK CLACKITY CLACK* on the front right side, and I jumped so high in fright I nearly punched a sun roof in the car. I feared the whole front end was coming apart and I'd be doomed in the middle of Wenatchee Avenue, having littered engine parts for at least two blocks. My problem was quickly repaired, however, when someone pulled off the hubcap and found that a loose tire bolt had come off and was rattling around inside.

I suspect our fears of motor noises are a carryover from childhood "monsters under the bed." Our adult tendencies to imagine worst-case scenarios from the mysteries of pistons and transmissions aren't much different from those little-squirt nightmares of bulgy-eyed, slimy things that wake up at bedtime and crawl out of the mattress. I'll confess I checked under my bed as a kid. Though I'd seen only dust bunnies, it didn't help at night to have an older sibling tease me with ominous noises!

My own children, thankfully, have not had too many problems with mattress monsters. I told them no monster could squeeze under their beds—they've got too much junk stored there. Besides, no monster would dare intrude when we begin the night with prayer.

I've learned that one way to get close to my children's hearts is to get on my knees by their beds. It's those mellow-talk-and-prayers-in-the-dark times—after the flurry of snacks, tooth brushing, and bedtime story—that I get closest to knowing my children. We'll talk about the day, what's ahead for tomorrow, and dare to share the things that bug them or scare them.

I think it's easier for them to talk when the darkness eliminates the need for eye contact and they know these problems will most likely be soon enfolded in prayer. Thus Inga talks about the "monster" of ice-skating lessons—how she just couldn't get the knack of skating on a certain edge of her blades. (Don't ask me to explain—I skate on two blades and my fanny.) And Zach airs his agony about trying to learn vibrato on the violin. Or we talk about frustrating teachers or classmates or siblings. I pray about their complaints, but I also pray for them to develop godly character qualities like patience, self-control, joy, and kindness—their best defense against the "monsters" they'll face all their lives.

I know, for part of my spiritual growth has required identifying "monsters" like those already examined in this book. I've had times of despair, reluctance, fear, bitterness, ingratitude, and discouragement. But my lowest times came when I was hit by the shroud of defeatism. I'm so much like the Israelites. Even when I've seen God be my helper and provider, there are times when my faith comes under the shadow of faithless monsters. I succumb to thinking that I am the inevitable victim of negative events.

That sort of thinking crept into the Israelite camp in the last half of Exodus 17. At Rephidim, just after God provided water from a rock, they were attacked by the Amalekites. Not since Pharaoh's army drowned in the Red Sea had they faced a human enemy and the possibility of war. Their crisis teaches us several things:

- We will always encounter enemies.
- Enemies attack where we are weakest.
- We can't win battles on our own strength.
- We need partners in prayer.
- We need to give God the glory for victory.

We'll Always Face Enemies

The Amalekites were the Hebrews' genetic cousins, offspring of Esau's son's concubine Timna (Gen. 36:12). Esau was the rebel of his family, the one who yielded easily to fleshly cravings, and his self-centeredness passed down to his descendants. The Amalekites roamed the Sinai as nomads. They were apprehensive of this mass of people invading their meager breadbasket.

We often think of enemies as forces outside ourselves. But they may also be our personal "monsters under the bed"—ugly critters like egotism, greed, anger, worry, or immoral habits. The uniforms of such enemies are often labeled "self."

One of my spiritual enemies has been self-righteous self-sufficiency. I thought my adult life would easily fall into place—job, house, marriage, that sort of thing. After all, hadn't God gotten me to adulthood with all my mind and limbs still functional? Then, during my senior year of college, I decided not to use the education degree I was earning. Instead of becoming a baby-faced high school English teacher, I went back to college for two more quarters of journalism, paid for by a summer cub reporter job. Unfortunately, I had picked a bad time to enter the battlefield called the Job Market. Cutbacks at Boeing, the Northwest's biggest employer, had depressed the entire economy in our area. I finally landed a summer-only job at a town whose name I couldn't even pronounce: Wenatchee. In midsummer they made my position permanent. I worked there nearly five years.

Years later and still single, with mission service behind me and a graduate degree nearly finished, God tested how well I'd learned to trust him as I knocked on more employers' doors. Again, a depressed economy affected the opportunities in my field. This time the enemy had me on my back, down to the last week before I had to vacate my student housing. My parents had died and I was without a car, 2,000 miles away from the storage bin holding my stuff. Early in the week, I interviewed for one position. I wasn't quite the person they wanted. But someone in another department was interested in me. By the end of the week, I had a job and a temporary housing offer—a mattress on the floor at somebody's home.

Did I still think myself invincibly self-sufficient? No way! At night, as I lay on that mattress, I thought of my past and my future with God. I acknowledged that I couldn't have achieved the basics of life—shelter, food, job—on my own. God had to provide. I thought of the classic hymn "May the Mind of Christ My Savior" and the line that says "I triumph only through his power." I remembered that the last verse had another *self* word: "May the love of Jesus fill me, as the waters fill the sea; him exalting, self-abasing, this is victory."

Victors love to flaunt their abilities and gains. But in God's eyes, we're winners when we humble ourselves before him. Self-abasement is the deliberate lowering of oneself before One who, out of love, lowered himself to die on a cross.

Enemies Attack Where We Are Weakest

But there are also enemies outside ourselves, like the Amalekites, who attack our weakest side. Deuteronomy 25:18 says this hateful tribe was so sneaky they preyed on the defenseless stragglers at the back: "When you were weary and worn out, they met you on your journey and cut off all who were lagging behind; they had no fear of God."

Such was the situation facing Elaine Bell, a single mother of two daughters. God had helped her through eight tough years of single parenting. But the enemy struck at her weakest point and hit her hard.

Elaine lived in an old, shabby house, but repairs were out of the question financially. Her divorce had left her responsible for a monthly house payment of $652, larger than the original mortgage because her former husband and she had consolidated other debts with the house as collateral. Added to that were debts from attending business school so she could better support her daughters. Even juggling bills, she couldn't keep up and faced a $500-a-month negative cash flow.

"I felt my situation was hopeless," Elaine says. "The loan manager of the credit union holding the existing mortgage had already stipulated that he would not consider refinancing until the house was repainted and re-roofed and had passed a foundation inspection."

The basement wall had cracks that seemed to be worsening. And even paint and a new roof wouldn't solve many of the house's problems. It would never pass inspection.

Built in the 1920s, the house had gone through haphazard remodeling that had turned its exterior into an ugly patchwork of four different types of surfacing material. "I was ashamed for people to know where I lived," Elaine says. "I even felt my shabby house tarnished my witness for Christ."

Moving wasn't an option. The house's problems would need to be fixed before it could be sold, and there was no decent housing available in her price range. Refinancing attempts at other banks proved futile.

We Can't Win on Our Own

When the Amalekites attacked from behind, Moses realized he had no choice but counterattack. He instructed Joshua to mobilize the fighting men and lead them into battle. It was not a pretty scene. War means blood, injuries, and death. But something else made this battle significant. Viewing the battle from a hill, Moses raised high the staff through which God had manifested multiple miracles. This was the walking stick that had turned into a snake before the elders and Pharaoh, called down plagues, parted the waters of the Red Sea, and broke a rock to quench a nation's thirst. Now that same staff remained in constant view of the Hebrew fighting men:

> As long as Moses held up his hands, the Israelites were winning, but whenever he lowered his hands, the Amalekites were winning. When Moses' hands grew tired, they took a stone and put it under him and he sat on it. Aaron and Hur held his hands up—one on one side, one on the other—so that his hands remained steady till sunset. So Joshua overcame the Amalekite army with the sword. (Exodus 17:11-13)

I know how tired my arms get when they're raised. Half an hour of violin practice, and my back and arms cry for relief. When I paint walls and ceilings, I climb off the ladder frequently to windmill my arms and knead out neck kinks. Surely greater exhaustion set in for an eighty-year-old man holding aloft a staff from sunrise to sunset, knowing its position determined the future of his people!

The Amalekite battle teaches that we cannot win conflicts on our own strength. Wisdom and power come from God alone. The staff we raise is the cross of Jesus Christ. When he is lifted up in our personal lives, he will be exalted in our public lives and will make a difference in the world.

God gave another picture of this principle in 2 Chronicles 20, when the armies of Judah withered as the Moabites and Ammonites assembled their massive forces. Judah's King Jehoshaphat prayed, admitting the enemy was too powerful to defeat without God's help. God ordered them to take their battle positions and then wait for him: "The battle is not yours, but God's" (2 Chron. 20:15). The morning of the battle, God must have scrambled the brains of the enemy, because they fought each other instead of Judah! Without losing a man, Judah won the battle.

As a writer, I constantly face two enemies with opposite temperaments. One is self-confidence; I think I can do anything handed me. The other is self-depreciation; I doubt my ability to start or finish anything worthy. The first is called pride; the second, writer's block! I prefer to face the writer's block, because it forces me to my knees by the desk, admitting I just don't know how to approach an article or chapter or story. I acknowledge that I can't do it without God's help. When I'm done confessing my inadequacies and claiming Christ's strength for what I have to do, God tells me to get up, wipe my tears, and get back on the keyboard. Bit by bit, the ideas and concepts come to me, and I realize again that it's God—not me—carrying the burden of writing.

Elaine's battle with her house confirmed that she was powerless to effect a change. But she knew God could work. Her need came to the attention of John, an insurance agent from her church who had contacted her as a possible client. John and his wife, Diana, decided to ask their Bible study to pray with Elaine for an alternate solution.

"The Lord led me back to my credit union, but this time by a back door," Elaine says. "One of the credit union's board members was a casual acquaintance. I approached him about my dilemma, asking if the board might make an exception for my case. Within days the credit union extended the mortgage repayment period, lowering my payment substantially—all without changeover fees!"

We Need Partners in Prayer

Moses' arms stayed up until the battle was over, thanks to Aaron and Hur. By holding up his weary arms, they participated in Moses' prayers for the Israelites to prevail. God allows—yes, even expects—others to participate in our personal prayer battles.

In Elaine's case, refinancing was only part of the problem. The project could have stopped there, but John and Diana and their Bible study group kept the staff raised. Now the group offered to paint and re-roof Elaine's house.

Prior to painting, they needed to correct the patchwork exterior. Elaine had no idea where to start. Then she got a phone call from another member of the Bible study. She'd noticed a classified ad placed by a man looking for asbestos siding to repair his mother's house. Most of Elaine's house was covered with that environmentally risky siding. Although three or four people had already called the man by the time Elaine phoned him, he chose to take her siding.

She next got a phone call from a stranger asking about buying her T1-11 siding, some of which she had in storage and some of which was on her house but very weathered. She hadn't even advertised it! But she learned how John's casual remark to another client about her project eventually reached someone who needed that type of siding. "My mouth dropped in amazement as he handed me the check for the siding," she says. "He generously paid me today's market price for it—even the weathered pieces!"

About this time, another Bible study from Elaine's church got involved with labor and finances. A man in one of the Bible studies was also a member of a Kiwanis organization. His club, for its outreach project, had just finished one roof project and was looking for another. Deciding that Elaine's roof qualified, they provided volunteers for the labor and paid part of the roofing price. A local roofing company donated the remaining supplies.

"Disposing of the old roofing could have cost close to $500," Elaine recalls, "but as volunteers started stripping off the three to four layers of peeling shingles, one care group member just backed up a truck bearing ten empty fruit bins. When they were full, he drove off and disposed of them."

More than twenty-five people were now involved in repairing Elaine's house. From June to October, people showed up on Saturday mornings to work on problems she couldn't afford to hire done or do herself. Elaine watched volunteers remove layers of roofing and siding, pull nails, scrape and sand peeling paint, fill in missing siding pieces, add trim to windows, and then apply a primer coat. A professional paint contractor sprayed on the final coat of paint. Others built storage shelves in her garage, did electrical improvements in the house, and properly ventilated her dryer. "I couldn't believe what God was doing through these people," Elaine remarks.

God has a wonderful way of raising up prayer partners and reminding us we're special to him. Several months before I finished graduate studies, I met two single librarians, Marty and Jinny, who were housemates. Outgoing and giving people, they took special interest in me when they learned my parents had just died. Often they invited me to their home to get perspective. I know they prayed for me.

Another time, I was touched how Anita and Peter Deyneka, leaders of a mission organization, took time out of their intense schedule to take me to lunch. We had mutual ties to my home area in Washington, but we had bigger ties to a compassionate God. I fought tears as they ended the meal by praying that God would dispel my discouragement and reveal his will. Those prayers mattered as graduation neared without prospect of a job. In my physical and mental exhaustion, the enemy called doubt tried to whisper the heresy that

God had forgotten me. But others' prayers helped me instead claim that "The Lord will accomplish what concerns me" (Ps. 138:8, NASB).

We Need to Give God the Glory

The battle didn't end with Joshua overcoming the Amalekites. Exodus 17:14 says God instructed Moses to write down the history of this battle. This is one of the few passages in Exodus (there are others in Numbers and Deuteronomy) where there is evidence of a nation's history being recorded at that time. The battle with the Amalekites really happened, and it's possible that Moses' record of the event partly motivated King Saul, hundreds of years later, to battle the Amalekites again.

That excites me. We believe in a God who is real. The Bible I used during my troubled months of job searching is marked with dates opposite certain verses. They remind me that God was there in the darkened auditorium of my life, waiting for the right time to push me onto the stage of his choosing.

Moses also built an altar at the battle site and gave it a name. In our downtown area we have civic art consisting of statues labeled with the title and artist's name. For a couple years we laughed every time we drove by one weird modern piece that showed only the bottom half of a human face. We gave it our own titles: "Cured Headache," "Seventh Grader in First Period Pre-Algebra," and "Bad Hair Day." Its real name didn't matter to us. But the name of Moses' altar was highly significant. He called it "YHWH Is My Banner."

The Hebrew soldiers didn't carry a literal banner into battle, but they carried the power of the most holy God, the One known only by his mystery name, too sacred to spell out, YHWH. In many translations it's rendered in small capitals: "the LORD." But it's literally the holy name the Israelites referred to only in their form of shorthand, out of awe and worship of who he is. When we face our own battles, we need to call on God, too, with holy reverence. We need to acknowledge that he is the One who goes before us, changing impossibilities into opportunities to glorify himself. And we need to tell others about his power, to encourage them no matter what enemies they face.

That's what I tell people who have tremendous stories of God's help but are hesitant to retell them lest they appear spiritually proud. Our testimonies may differ in content, but when they proclaim that the Lord is our banner, they bring glory to God. And that pleases him.

That's how I convinced Elaine to tell her story. Her house project was an unforgettable illustration of God's power. The testimony didn't go unnoticed, as businessmen needing a "club project" hammered and painted alongside her Christian friends whose only service motivation was to serve the King of kings. The experience also touched the lives of her two daughters—one just out of high school and one in middle school. Most importantly, it affected Elaine's spiritual walk.

"It helped me grow spiritually in regard to my own stewardship," Elaine says. "I recommitted my life to Christ after my marriage, but my husband wasn't a Christian and he wasn't interested in giving to the church. After our separation and divorce, I wanted to give more to the Lord. But my debts were so great that when I tried to tithe, I'd get in a pinch with the bill collectors. Still, I'd feel guilty when the offering was collected during the service and I couldn't put something in." Her church offered her some financial counseling. That guidance plus a sermon on the widow and her mite (Luke 21:1-4) challenged Elaine toward a more consistent giving pattern. Eventually she was able to achieve her goal of tithing her income.

"Now when I pull in my driveway," she says, "I breathe a prayer of thanks. I'm reminded of Matthew 6:33, where Jesus said we should seek first his kingdom and his righteousness, then 'all these things'—meaning all living needs—'will be given to you as well.' Who but God could have coordinated all these things to solve a problem that I had nearly given up on?"

Defeatism gives up because it leaves God out of the battle. God wants us to continue praying for people or circumstances until we see his answer. When we take the Lord's banner into battle—when we face our enemies with prayer and anticipation—we'll find victory especially sweet.

I remember that as I lie on my current mattress. This one, thankfully, isn't on the floor! But as I look to the wall on my left, I see an 11 x 14 enlargement of a daffodil, a wedding gift from a friend and amateur photographer. I use that photo as a reminder to pray for him, because ten years after he took that picture he went from a prominent business position to imprisonment for murder. Enemies such as self-worship, self-righteousness, and self-indulgence have landed him at the bottom. But I believe the promise of Isaiah 59:1: "Surely the arm of the Lord is not too short to save, nor his ear too dull to hear." I am praying that this man will humble himself before God and be set free from the prison of sin by receiving Jesus into his life. I also continue to pray for the family members affected by his crime. And I know others pray, too. We're holding up each other's arms in anticipation of a very special victory.

Mileposts

1. Grab a dictionary and look up the *self* words. List some that reflect the spiritual enemies you face. What does Galatians 5:17 say about these enemies?
2. Read Romans 6:11-14. What truths does it present for dealing with spiritual enemies?
3. Recall a time when you really felt defeated and beaten down. How might Ephesians 3:16 have helped?
4. Compare Psalm 138:8 with Isaiah 26:12. What message of hope do they share?
5. The book of Isaiah is a symphony of dark and light, contrasting a nation's sin and God's promise to renew. The following passage has helped encourage many people in their darkest days. You'll be glad you memorized

it: "Do not fear, for I am with you; do not be dismayed, for I am your God. I will strengthen you and help you; I will uphold you with my righteous right hand" (Isa. 41:10).

I wait for the Lord, my soul waits,
and in his word I put my hope.—Psalm 130:5

8
Are We There Yet?

Impatience and Self-control

I analyze humankind at stoplights.

The guy ahead of me, hugging the crosswalk line, is Donald Destination. His motto is, "Put the pedal to the metal." He strains to see the crosswise signals turn yellow, his foot poised to spread rubber. He dreams of turning his car into a helicopter and lifting right out of red lights, traffic jams, and other inconveniences. To put it mildly, Donald is rather impatient with anything that gets in his way.

Then there's Carol Carpool. Passengers are her entire reason for going somewhere. She gets 22,000 words to the gallon. She loves stop lights, for they allow her more opportunities to comment on new cars, interesting pedestrians, and the fashions in the J. C. Penney window. Carol loves to try new ways of getting to work or the mall. Often she gets lost, but that's half the fun of driving. Carol is impatient with people who don't take the time to enjoy life.

Next meet Michael Map. For the past twenty-three years, Michael has taken the same route to work and the grocery store, having determined that those routes take the least time and gas. He also knows that the stoplights at certain intersections last twenty seconds, and that if he drives at twenty-seven miles per hour he will be able to hit all of them green. Michael gets distressed and impatient around Don and Carol. He cannot understand why they are so focused or so disorganized.

Finally, here comes Evie Eventually. Like Michael, she tends to drive the same route. But she doesn't mind if she has to go twenty-five miles out of her way to take a dinner to somebody who's been sick. She'll still make it to choir practice, give or take a half hour. Red lights don't trouble her too much. Evie has a lot of patience, but she causes other drivers to lose theirs.

On the highway to heaven, we often have Donald and Michael behind Carol and Evie. No wonder it gets crazy at times! But sometimes God makes us wait for things that are really worthwhile.

I think about that in my own life. I didn't marry until age thirty-four. By that time I was ready to twist my hair into a neckline bun, buy seven ankle-length navy dresses, and invest in orthopedic shoes that would last me the next twenty years. (Don't you believe it.) But I had concluded that marriage wasn't God's agenda for me. Then, when it came, my intended gave me six weeks to get ready so we could be wed before he started his next year of teaching. That included my moving 2,000 miles. Patience? Well, you decide!

Our next lesson in patience (or lack thereof) surfaced five months into our marriage, when I experienced flu symptoms and backaches that nothing could cure. The light slowly dawned over the next eight months as I went from a svelte bride to a whale who kept whining, "Is it due yet?" I got so big that I had to use the handicapped stalls at restrooms. The only one not in a hurry for the blessed event was the whale calf, who was happily swimming in its amniotic sea.

Of course, birth brings its own bag of lessons in patience. And as the kids grow up, you have many opportunities to learn a lot more about patience. For one thing, kids don't have any. Anyone who doubts that should just say "Christmas" to a child in early December and see how many times a day one gets asked, "Is it Christmas yet?" No, sweetie, it's not Christmas yet.

So often we're like little children. We want a raise, and we want it now. We want a new house, new car, better church—and we don't want to wait for God. He moves too slowly.

Yet God's timing is always right. When we settle for instant answers, we settle for something that's considerably less than his best. That's what happened as the Hebrews left Rephidim, where they saw God provide just what they needed once they admitted they couldn't succeed on their own. They next went to Sinai, the mountain of God, where he provided them with ten laws the world has never improved on. There, another problem surfaced. Though Israel had been taken out of Egypt, "Egypt" had not been taken out of Israel. Exodus 32 tells of harsh lessons for those of us prone to impatience:

- Waiting can bring out the worst in us.
- It's easy to fall back into old habits.
- We can't hide from God.
- God's patience spares us.
- Godly patience means self-control.

Waiting Brings Out the Worst

The average person will wait for an elevator forty seconds before becoming visibly agitated.[11] "An old Chinese proverb observes: "He who plants a tree in the morning wants to saw planks from it at evening." We've all seen those little plaques that say, "I want patience, and I want it right now!"

Impatience has been around ever since Eve wouldn't wait to check out Satan's story about the forbidden fruit. The journeying Hebrews fell into the same trap when Moses disappeared into the ominous cloud shrouding Mt. Sinai a second time to meet with God. The first time he'd brought down laws governing how the people would live (Ex. 20-23). During this second meeting, God was giving Moses a blueprint for worship based on the model of heaven itself. But after forty days of not seeing their earthly leader, the Hebrews lost patience.

"As for this fellow Moses who brought us up out of Egypt, we don't know what has happened to him," they scoffed. You can hear their contempt in *"this fellow* Moses." With impatience they decided to turn away from God and pursue the type of religion they knew from Egypt. They were dancing around a bovine idol when Moses came down from the presence of the holy God of the universe.

The scene was proof of how waiting can weaken our resolve, stoke our disobedience, and blind us to commitments. New Christians are especially vulnerable to similar temptations. After experiencing the miraculous change of spiritual rebirth, they want to charge ahead. God wants them to pause and grow, taking the time to nurture inner change. They want the spectacular, the signs and wonders that set their adrenaline in overdrive and make God more exciting than New Years Eve in Times Square or half time at the Super Bowl. God wants them to wait at the stoplights until he's ready to move.

Nobody enjoys those stoplights. A friend I'll call Ann came to one after growing up in a legalistic church that portrayed God as a judge, not as a loving Father. She feared she'd never be good enough for heaven. After she married and became a mother, she worried about whether her children could get to heaven, too.

Ann sought answers in religious books and other churches. Sadly, one minister couldn't even explain how a person could be assured of going to heaven. At another church, which stressed the Bible instead of tradition, she plied the minister and others with questions about their practices. From a Christian friend she heard the truth that going to heaven depended on accepting Christ as Savior, not on rituals or church laws. Then someone gave her a copy of the then-new *Living Bible* paraphrase. She plunged into it, spiritually ravenous.

"I couldn't believe the simplicity of salvation," she says. "It could happen anywhere, anytime. For me, it happened one night as I was alone in bed reading in John 4 about the woman at the well. She was just like me, thinking she had to have special places to worship. But Jesus said she only needed to worship in spirit and in truth. That was it—just me and Jesus. I dropped to my knees and gave my life to him."

Ann immersed herself in her Bible, sometimes reading it by the hour and making lists of questions and answers. She took the Bible at times so literally that, for example, reading in Matthew 6:6 (KJV) about going into a prayer closet, she slipped into a coat closet to pray. After her conversion, both her children eventually asked Christ into their lives.

"My husband's faith would make us complete," she says. But the healthy, handsome athlete she'd married had changed completely. A self-proclaimed agnostic, he'd become a solitary drinker, prone to long silences and unexplained absences.

"For three years I prayed for him," she recalls. "Oh, how I prayed. I had read books about being unequally yoked and envisioned how, someday, God would work a miracle in his life. But the deeper I walked with Christ, the further this man withdrew. One day he calmly announced his intention to end our fourteen-year marriage. He said he no longer loved me and he was moving out. Just like that. He showed no emotion, but I felt like I'd been slammed by a freight train."

Falling Back into Old Ways

At first Ann responded to her fears by listening to Christian music, praying, and reading her Bible. She told her children that they would all trust God to help them through this.

"I fantasized that Philemon 15 would be a message to me," she says. "That verse says, 'Perhaps the reason he was separated from you for a little while was that you might have him back for good.' I daydreamed about him some day coming back, taking me in his arms, kissing me tenderly, and summoning the children in a tearful, loving reconciliation."

Instead, over the next few months he became increasingly hostile toward Ann and the children. He withheld money and filed for divorce, threatening her if she refused to meet his conditions.

"My Christian friends seemed to pull away from me," she said. "I felt isolated, lonely, and scared. Worse, I started to doubt God. Could he love me and still let me twist in the wind like this? Was this how he rewarded those who entrusted their lives to him? Or was the whole idea of being a Christian just a cruel hoax designed to hook luckless fools like me?"

Then her ex-husband married the woman with whom he'd apparently been having a long-time affair. Besides a broken heart, Ann was left with two children, a derelict car, a mortgage, no education, and an oppressive load of fear.

"I was so hurt by his betrayal that my behavior didn't reflect my commitment to God," Ann says. "My anger grew and my spirit sank. In my confusion and isolation, I began to lose my spiritual bearings. I stopped praying regularly and reading my Bible. I lapsed into worldly bitterness and complaining, starting old destructive habits again."

Here Ann's life paralleled the impatient Hebrews as they asked Aaron to make them an idol. Most texts label this idol as a calf, but the Hebrew term really denotes a young bull in his first strength. In both Egyptian and Canaanite religions, the bull represented strength and reproductive power. Perhaps Aaron thought it could represent the great strength of Jehovah. But it was an affront to the God who had just told them to worship only him and to make no idols to represent him. The people weren't connecting with God. Instead, they connected with their Egyptian heritage and their base desires as they "worshiped" in sensuous revelry.

Scripture is clear that Christians need to shed old habits and take on new, godly lifestyles. Romans 12:2 says we must allow God to renew our thought processes and desires. Sometimes he makes those changes very obvious! A friend told how he kept playing in nightclub bands after he became a Christian, focusing on bringing in extra money to support his family. When he asked his pastor if he should continue this, the pastor wisely said, "Pray about it." He knew that decision had to come from within this new believer. The man said his next engagement was a disaster. Band members didn't show up. His amplifier didn't work. Drunks hung on him. He finally got the message that this wasn't where a Christian belonged. He put an ad in the paper for his bass guitar and amplifier and sold them the same day the ad came out.

Many people wrongly think Christianity is a list of do's and don'ts. Yes, the Bible gives us standards for living, but they're navigational aids. "God gave us rules not to keep us in bondage but to guide us to liberty and fullness," writes LeRoy Eims. When God gave Moses the Ten Commandments, he first said, "I am the LORD your God, who brought you out of Egypt, out of the land of slavery" (Ex 20:2). As Eims notes, "The laws he gave us were intended to keep his people out of slavery to sin, to self, to tyranny."[12] Our problem is that we often don't recognize what enslaves us. We make excuses for our choices until we have a crisis encounter with God.

We Can't Hide from God

The perennial parent-child vegetable wars often result in some sort of cover-up work by the child. Dinner comes and with it those dreaded orders, "No leaving the table until you've eaten your broccoli." The child who sweetly asks, "May I please be excused?" and whose plate is neatly covered with a napkin may have unconfessed sin. It's funny how lumpy concealed vegetables can be!

The Hebrews acted just like that when they decided to dance the polka around their golden barnyard animal. Even though God was busy giving Moses the Ten Commandments, he still had an eye on what was happening below.

God knew what was going on in Ann's heart, too, and heard her when her deepening misery climaxed one lonely night in her living room.

"I finally unleashed my fury," she remembers, "and screamed aloud at God. Here I'd trusted him with my life, my children, everything. In what seemed the ultimate betrayal, it seemed he'd stomped my dreams to dust." Ann yelled and sobbed as she released that anger. Then, completely spent, she lay numbly on the sofa.

"As I lay there testing my raw feelings, I realized I felt no shame," she says. "My anger melted away as the gentle words of Romans 8:28 echoed repeatedly through my soul—that all this would work together for good to those who loved God and were called according to his purpose. My feeble faith could hardly grasp the impact of those words. But somehow I knew, despite all my agony, that God was still my loving Father. My long-simmering anger hadn't caught him by surprise. He knew me inside and out. Hiding my disillusionment had been foolish."

God's Patience Spares Us

When God saw that the Israelites had turned their backs on him, he prepared to turn his back on them. Instead of "My" people, he told Moses they were "your" people (Ex. 32:7) and "these people" (v. 9). He was tired of how they acted like stubborn oxen and were now so smitten by their golden bull that they were "running wild," "out of control," and "a laughingstock to their enemies" (v. 25). God was ready to destroy them all and start over with Moses to build a nation to inhabit the Promised Land. But Moses pleaded for a second chance. The God of Second Chances gave it.

Often we, too, write off people as hopeless. We think they're so far from God that nothing can change them. But we shortchange the depths of God's love when we make that evaluation. At the top of our prayer lists we should write this verse: "He is patient with you, not wanting anyone to perish, but everyone to come to repentance" (2 Pet. 3:9).

God yearns to have his children return his love. His greatest desire is reconciliation. But there will always be those who refuse him. Moses' return to camp resulted in a stern and bloody roll call for loyalty. "Whoever is for the Lord, come to me," Moses shouted (v. 26). All the Levites responded, obeying Moses' command to execute those who'd turned from God.

The prospects of living apart from God eternally should chill us to the bone. This is the heart of evangelism. Not only should we yearn to be in fellowship with God, we should desire it for others. It's so easy to get wrapped up in our holy huddles, enjoying Christian fellowship with like-minded people. But God sent us into the world to be his agents of change. People are dancing around their own idols out there. They don't know any better. As Frances Havergal wrote in her classic hymn "Who Is on the Lord's Side?":

> Who is on the Lord's side? Who will serve the King?
> Who will be his helpers, Other lives to bring?
> Who will leave the world's side? Who will face the foe?
> Who is on the Lord's side? Who for him will go?

It only takes a few steps to move from murmuring to impatience to idolatry. But it's not a one-way street. The mercy of God enables us to return to him when we realize that our idols are empty and we want to continue the journey with him alone.

The night Ann screamed at God was her spiritual turning point. Drained of anger, she got back into her *Living Bible*, underlining passages that comforted and reassured her.

"Psalm 32:8 reminded me that God would instruct me and guide me along the best pathway," Ann recalls. "He'd advise me and watch my progress. I needed to know that. I also needed that psalm's verse 10: 'Abiding love surrounds those who trust in the Lord.' I rejoiced in Psalm 34:17-18: 'Yes, the Lord hears the good man when he calls to him for help, and saves him out of all his troubles. The Lord is close to those whose hearts are breaking.' I came to Daniel 10:19 and said 'that's me' as I underlined it: 'God loves you very much . . .

don't be afraid! Calm yourself; be strong—yes, strong.'"

As Ann's faith moved forward, she met someone else who could walk alongside. "Kind, thoughtful, warm, generous, and also touched by divorce, he shared not only my pain but also my hope in Jesus," she says. "We were married, and from our hurts has come a ministry to divorced and remarried people and their families. I've also had the joy of watching my grown children establish Christian homes."

Patience and Self-control

Before writing this book, I wrote one titled *When I Prayed for Patience . . . God Let Me Have It.* Now that book is coming back to haunt me! If I get upset with my family, they'll retort, "Sure, Mom, and you wrote the book on patience!" But one point of my book is that patience is a lifelong learning process. God calls us to train to be patient: "Make every effort to add to your faith goodness; and to goodness, knowledge; and to knowledge, self-control; and to self-control, perseverance; and to perseverance, godliness" (2 Pet. 1:5-6).

We should desire most deeply to become more godly in every area of our lives. And we should never forget that God won't turn his back on us until we have utterly, irrevocably turned our backs on him. Ann remembers that as she recalls the night she screamed at God. "I'm grateful that his infinite love embraced even my anger," she says. "He's still transforming me, especially in regard to fear and worry, my worst weaknesses. But I don't need to scream at the ceiling. I've experienced how God can turn suffering into good. My suffering didn't come from him, but he covered it with his nail-pierced hand to redeem it—and me.

"It was a long journey from my darkest days. Some days I wondered if I could wait for God any longer. I couldn't handle his silence. But the whole, heart-wrenching experience showed me the truth of Romans 5:3-5. My suffering taught me patience and developed my character. And from that came a rock-solid hope in God that nothing can take away."

We show we are learning self-control through our obedience. Aaron failed that test when he got so caught up in pleasing the people that he took his tools and made an idol. He even tried to cover it up, telling Moses, "I threw [the gold] into the fire, and out came this calf!" The more we practice self-control, the more we'll understand the heart of God.

Southern Utah contains numerous slot canyons, formed by crevasses in the sandstone hundreds of feet deep and sometimes only two or three feet wide. Many are grouped in such confusing ways they act like a maze. One October day in 1996 a hiker started on a day trek but got confused. He searched all day for the way out, squeezing through some canyons on his side. Finally, he got wedged in a narrow crevasse. He had three bites of sandwich and five ounces of water left. After the first day, he rationed his water—one sip a day. He spent eight long, hot days and shivery nights stuck and helpless. He'd think hours had passed, when his watch told him only fifteen or twenty minutes had slipped by.

A worried friend launched search parties. The afternoon of the eighth day, the hiker heard the faint tinkle of a bell on a search dog's collar. Rescuers heard the hiker's weak yell and got him out. "People stand in a line at a grocery store and get mad after five minutes," he says now. "Never me. Never again."[13]

Sometimes God needs to put us in a place where all we can do is wait. Stuck at a red light, we begin to see our impatience as he sees it. When we finally get a green light, we head on our way—changed. Not perfect, though. We're still vulnerable to forgetfulness, the challenge of the next chapter.

Mileposts

1. Someone once said, "You can accomplish just about anything if you have patience. You can even carry water in a sieve if you wait for it to freeze." How is that true in the spiritual realm? What help can you get from Isaiah 30:18?
2. Sometimes it only takes a few steps to go from murmuring

to idolatry. Review the "golden calf" incident through the perspective of Psalm 106:19-23. What problems might we have in common with the Israelites?

3. Was Sinai the end of Israel's problem with idols? Read 1 Kings 12 and tell what amazing thing happened. Then fast-forward 300 years and touch down in the reign of King Josiah (2 Kings 23) and see what occupied his reign. What things in our lives might be equally difficult to eradicate?

4. The idols of our culture revolve around pleasure. We don't bow to them but we allow them to occupy our thoughts, pull at our passions, and invade our checkbooks. What does Romans 6:5-14 reveal about coming under their control?

5. God's Word can be powerful in its simplicity. The heart of this chapter's lesson is easy to memorize: "Dear children, keep yourselves from idols" (1 John 5:21).

But who can endure the day of his coming?
Who can stand when he appears?
For he will be like a refiner's fire.
—*Malachi 3:2*

9
Where There's Smoke There's Ire

Forgetfulness and Remembrance

Here in central Washington we have our own version of the old rural saying, "Lord willin' and the creek don't rise." For us it's "Lord willin' and the pass don't close." Between us and big-time civilization (the Seattle-Tacoma urban sprawl) are the Cascade Mountains, which skiers love and cross-state drivers endure during the winter. We can usually count on one or two abominable snowstorms per winter to cripple east-west travel.

I'm not complaining. This area we call the "Apple Capital of the World" is spared a lot of nature's wrath. We did choke through ash-fall of the 1980 eruption of Mount St. Helens. But we don't have California-style earthquakes, though long ago one triggered a slide which plugged the Columbia River. Forget blizzards—this is technically high desert. Most of the snow gets dumped in the mountains. During spring thaw, dams on the Columbia River tame its floods. And we shipped all our tornados to the Midwest! Our problem is summer fires.

None of us will forget the big ones of 1995, when hot stuff this time closed the passes that link us to life "on the other side." The fires began one July night after a long heat wave, when lightning strafed over thousands of acres, turning forests into furnaces. By the fifth day, flames from three major fires had rampaged over rural homes, shrouded the valley in smoke, and churned over hills toward our town. Firefighters from twenty-five states arrived to fight the inferno. Then came the unnerving announcement: our area of town, close to the hills, was on Level 1 alert. We were to be ready for evacuation.

Those are times you wish you drove a moving van instead of a compact car. Besides our family of four we were responsible for my husband's mother and invalid father plus an invalid uncle across town. We realized we could take little besides ourselves, and that if we did have to leave, we might come home to ashes. We knew how fast and explosive fire could be. A few years earlier, kids playing with matches on a windy day set off a blaze that took only minutes to incinerate an entire neighborhood of homes just blocks away. Three families we knew lost everything.

Grandma had a suitcase of medicines ready. My then ten-year-old daughter looked sadly at her overflowing Barbie doll play corner. Her brother, almost twelve, went to his room for one "last play" with his cache of Legos.

Mercifully, the fires never reached our town, though they blackened 182,000 acres and destroyed more than 100 homes and outbuildings. They cost nearly $70 million to suppress. They also closed off the mountain passes. It was several weeks before we could drive through the still-smoldering mountain landscape, where temporary signs warned of possible burning material falling off cliffs.

Our fires of '95 were bad, though not as historically significant as those in places like Rome, Chicago, San Francisco, or even Kuwait. But a fire doesn't have to be big to be important. Numbers 11 records the small scrubland fire at Taberah which represented these major spiritual lessons:

- We'll all face unexpected spiritual tests.
- Complaining reveals our spiritual condition.
- Self-indulgent cravings displease God.
- God is patient and generous as we respond to him.

Expect the Unexpected

Appropriately, one Old Testament thinker used a fire analogy as he struggled to explain why bad things happen to presumably "good" people. "Man is born to trouble," said Job's talkative comforter Eliphaz, "as surely as sparks fly upward" (Job 5:7). Nobody escapes life without enduring times of hardship. Trouble always has a cause. Sometimes suffering comes from bad choices we make. We reap what we sow. Other times we suffer because we all share in the consequences of man's separation from God. Sometimes our suffering, as it was for Job, is a deliberate scheme of Satan to drive a wedge between us and God.

This side of heaven, we'll never have a satisfactory answer for why hardships come and why certain ones come to us. But we can learn from the ways people respond to suffering. Some holler so loudly that the problem seems a lot worse than it is. When my children were small, they sometimes played a little roughly, and invariably one would proclaim the "hardship" with loud and mournful wails. After checking to make sure the victim was still conscious and walking, I usually solved the problem with an ice cube wrapped in a wash cloth!

But it's another thing when life knocks us flat. In the midst of writing this book, my family experienced a spiritual fire on a snowy Oregon pass. We were on our way home from a weekend trip in October. We hadn't gotten away during the summer, partly because we'd paid off our daughter's orthodontic bill and couldn't afford much. Stress had taken a toll on our communication. Taking advantage of a school holiday, we'd looked forward to a long weekend to re-connect as a family. About 8 P.M. Saturday we had just gotten over the summit of a 4,700-foot mountain pass in blowing, wet snow. As a family we said aloud, "Thank you, Lord," for answering fervent prayers for safety. We knew we'd soon be out of snow. My husband, Rich, had geared down for control as we crept downhill in the ruts left by previous vehicles. Noticing headlights around the next bend, I said, "Watch out!" Rich reacted by pulling to the shoulder and in the next split second our lives were changed.

A sickening thud, the crinkle of glass, and we sat in a crumpled car whipped sideways. I looked in the back seat and saw my son, dazed and bloodied from window glass shredding his face, his front teeth broken. Blood also trickled down his dad's face. Our night of agony in an emergency room included hearing of alleged alcohol involvement. It hurt the next day to see our well cared-for family car towed to a junkyard. That night, three hundred miles later, I wept as we safely pulled into our driveway in a rented car.

A week later came another "thud"—the news that my husband's newly widowed mother had cancer.

As we pulled together as a family, we acknowledged that we weren't the first to face difficulties. Among our Christian friends is Earl Carey, a servant-hearted man whose gracious manner gives no hint of the devastating hardship he experienced in a business failure. His story in many ways parallels that of Numbers 11—but has a different ending.

Earl grew up knowing about God. He was the fourth of six children born to a postmaster in a small Washington community. He always admired how his dad lived his walk with God, and he knew his mother was a prayer warrior. Earl was a "good kid." At ten he started helping his father around the post office. When Earl was a high school sophomore, his father became seriously ill, and Earl dropped out of school to take over. Even as a teenager he impressed a postal inspector. "I was too young to know I should be afraid of his visit," Earl recalls. "He found only three or four minor deficiencies in the operation. Was I proud to take that report home to Dad."

Earl's diligence pleased his parents, but there was one part of his life that he hadn't yet settled. When he left home for the army and business college, he hadn't yet asked Christ into his life. He was working as a meat cutter when his dad asked him to come home and help at the post office. Within a day of Earl's arrival, his father died of a heart attack.

"I was twenty," Earl recalls. "I knew I wasn't following Christ. I wouldn't see my dad again in heaven unless I made a change."

Complaints and Saints

All of the people in the Israelite camp had been "saved" from slavery in Egypt. But not all of them truly knew and obeyed the God who was leading them to a better land. Numbers 10:33 reveals they were three days down the road from their extended stop below Mt. Sinai. That's where they had received the Ten Commandments and had initiated a worship pattern designed by God. They had all they needed to become God's holy and obedient people. Yet they grew lax spiritually.

Unfortunately, people today think the same way. They presume a previous encounter with God will "vaccinate" them against problems. It's tempting logic. I deliberately exposed my children to chicken pox in the days before a vaccine was available for that pesky disease. I was sixteen when I had chicken pox, and "miserable" doesn't begin to describe my three weeks of illness. I didn't want them to experience "hard pox" as teens, so one summer day I arranged a friendly visit with the latest pox-infested friend. "Hug him real good," I urged as they shared toys and pox viruses. My scheme worked—sort of. Zach got sick, but not Inga. She waited to get it from Zach. I had a whole month of chicken pox in the house! But I counted my blessings. They wouldn't get it again!

Life and pox are not the same. God may make himself real to us through a dramatic salvation experience or a close-call episode. But as time fades that memory, we may let our spiritual life slide. We may slack off attending church or let prayer and Bible reading grow stale. That's what happened to the Hebrews. They had ample evidence that God cared for them. What could top the Passover of the Angel of Death and the crossing of the Red Sea? The guiding pillar of fire? The miraculous provisions of water, manna, and quail? Victory over vicious enemies? In spite of their dramatic spiritual encounters with God, the Hebrews let three weary days on the trail overshadow God's love—and they complained.

The word *complained* in Numbers 11:1 is different from the usual word we encounter about the peoples' negative reactions. This one literally means "to sigh habitually." This reminds me of Eeyore, the donkey in A. A. Milne's Winnie the Pooh stories. Eeyore was well known for sighing "Oh dear" whenever something (usually anything) didn't go his way. The biblical text doesn't specify the Hebrews' grievance list, but it does say they complained in the Lord's hearing. They wanted him to hear them grumble, "We can't stand it any longer." They'd had it with the desert and with wandering around.

God heard, but was displeased: "When he heard them his anger was aroused. Then fire from the Lord burned among them and consumed some of the outskirts of the camp." Notice that the complainers were on the outskirts of the camp, away from the Ark of the Covenant and its visual reminder of the presence of a holy God. They illustrated how the further we are from God, the easier it is to disobey him and to complain.

When Earl's life was rocked by his dad's sudden death, he knew he had to close the distance between himself and God. That week, guided by his family's pastor, Earl put his faith in Christ. Earl was serious about his faith and about his vocation. He was eventually appointed to his father's post, married, and became the father of three daughters. Earl and his wife, Nadeen, appreciated his job security and were heavily involved in their church. Earl had also built up a successful insurance agency. Everything seemed to be "just right." But after thirteen years, Earl and his wife felt their three musically gifted daughters had needs their small town couldn't satisfy.

Friends couldn't understand their decision to leave when everything seemed to be going so well. But God had a reason to move them out. From the perspective of several decades, Earl wonders now if one reason might have been that he was relying too much on his own abilities—for with the move came the greatest spiritual test of his life.

Craving and Raving

The Hebrews knew the fire of God could rampage through the entire camp and exterminate all of them.

When they cried out to Moses, he prayed, and God quelled the flames. But again they forgot. The stench of smoke probably still hung in their clothes when they complained again, this time about the food: "The rabble with them began to crave other food and again the Israelites started wailing and said, 'If only we had meat to eat! We remember the fish we ate in Egypt at no cost—also the cucumbers, melons, leeks, onions and garlic. But now we have lost our appetite; we never see anything but this manna!'" (Num. 11:4-6).

The *rabble* consisted of strangers who'd joined the Israelites in the flight from Egypt. These people didn't necessarily believe in Israel's God but took the chance to leave oppression. They started mumbling and grumbling, and soon the Israelites caught their tune. They acted just like spoiled children, disgruntled employees, bored sports fans, impatient shoppers, tired students . . . and forgetful believers. When everybody's doing it, it's so easy to join in. The problem is that we mistake a few for "everybody." The people with whom we associate can influence our reactions for bad. They can encourage us to crave what is wrong—to focus on stomach-size, not soul-size, issues.

Yet God often calls us to stand alone. Maybe it's reminding our lunchroom partners that complaining about the boss behind his back won't help the situation. Or maybe it's being like salt in the family get-together—the one who refuses to put down others or spread gossip. Perhaps it's rejecting fashion trends if they carry wrong messages about sexuality. We may need to turn off the TV or radio talk shows and refuse to give a platform to people extoling "alternate lifestyles." We may just have to say, "Sorry, that's not for me," when a fellow Christian suggests an action we see as contrary to God's Word.

Earl's life journey took him into such choices. After working a few years for the state, he bought a business from a Christian friend. Before long, Earl and Nadeen realized the friend hadn't revealed all the problems that came with the business. It became an experience that burned them. Sometimes when problems became so monumental, they'd call a family meeting and just pray. Even when they couldn't see the answer, they knew they needed to trust God to work it out. In this case, however, God didn't work things out as they desired. Despite long hours and personal sacrifice, the business failed, and they suffered a large financial loss. Many, including fellow believers, urged the Careys to sue. But Earl and Nadeen committed the matter to prayer and, unlike the Hebrews, decided not to let the crowd influence their decision for God.

"We were disillusioned," Earl says, "but God used it to teach us to trust Him. We were concerned for the image of Christians which a lawsuit would convey to those outside the church. It just didn't seem what God would have us do."

God's Extraordinary Patience

The Hebrews' complaints distressed Moses, who felt the burden of each negative word. After all he had done, it wasn't enough. He was ready to give up and die. But God ignored Moses' request and instead appointed seventy elders to lighten Moses' leadership burden. Then he sent the meat they requested. The sky darkened with migrating quail, but the meat carried a plague. The map of their journey acquired another dismal name, "Kibroth Hattaavah," graves of craving, as they left their dead behind.

Numbers 11 is a distressing chapter, for it seems to show no spiritual progress. Twice the people railed against God, and twice they were judged. Forgetfulness cloyed their relationship with the Lord who had done so much for them already. He only wanted them to remember what they had come through and how he had helped them—and to use that as the basis for trusting him to get them to the Promised Land.

We don't need to wander in Sinai to apply that lesson to our lives. Every person's biography includes at least one fire chapter—and those are the times God asks us to remember how he has helped us in the past. They are also the times he asks us to examine our own reactions and motives. In his classic devotional study, *The Calvary Road,* Roy Hession sketches those times of examination as a journey to the highway which Isaiah 35:8 calls the "Way of Holiness." Getting to the highway requires ascending a hill so steep and forbidding that we have to crawl there on our hands and knees—especially our knees, the posture for prayer. That climb ends at the top of the hill, where there is a cross, and, at its foot, a door so low we have to stoop to crawl through it. Hession calls this place "the Door of the Broken Ones," for it accommodates only those whose spirits have been broken to the point of saying, "not I, but Christ":

> Before we can enter the Highway, God must bend and break that stiff-necked self, so that Christ reigns in its stead. To be broken means to have no rights before God and man. It does not mean merely surrendering my rights to Him but rather recognizing that I haven't any, except to deserve hell. It means just being nothing and having nothing that I call my own, neither time, money, possessions, nor position.[14]

The key to remembering God's mercies is acknowledging that we deserve none of them. When we go through fires of suffering, we are stripped down to our awareness that absolutely nothing matters outside our relationship with God. We need to claim the truth that the track record of his past mercies is the promise of his future ones.

While the failure of Earl and Nadeen's business represented a significant loss, they affirm that God continued to show his patience and love toward them. "At times I wondered why God allowed us to go through that mess," Earl says. "But when I look back, I realize how much the business consumed us physically and emotionally. It affected the time I spent with God and the priority I placed on family life."

Freed of the business's emotional and physical drain, Earl found himself spending more quality time with his girls. He also saw God bless another business, a taxi cab company and service station, which he bought. And he will never forget the counsel and encouragement he got from his pastor as he sorted out his feelings and continued to seek the will of God. "Our pastor helped us keep our spirits in tune with God," Earl says. "He desired more than anything that Nadeen and I be united on any decision we made. That was so important to us."

One day a local businessman unexpectedly walked into their service station with an offer to buy them out.

"We hadn't even put up a for-sale sign," Earl says, "although I had started to think about changing careers. We were doing well, but it was also a 24-hour-a-day, every day, responsibility. I was still able to work sixty to eighty hours a week, but I couldn't do that many more years. I also thought of my family's financial future. I already had fifteen years of government service. If I could somehow get in another five, I would have retirement benefits."

The business sold in thirty days, and Earl went job-hunting. He went to the post office, counting on his previous career there to put him back on its payroll. Instead, he met opposition. He could only come in at the bottom as a substitute letter carrier, a job usually assigned to young men, not those nearly fifty. It didn't matter that he'd once been a postmaster. The system didn't allow him to jump back to management.

Earl took a route anyway, hoping for promotions to put him back behind the counter. After being promoted and honored several times, he decided to try again for a postmaster job. Thirteen times he was passed over.

In 1985 another opening was announced in Rock Island, a town of about 1,000, within driving distance of his home. Again, Earl and Nadeen prayed as he went to the interview. This time, he got it.

"God knew what was best," Earl says. "We didn't have to move, and he needed me in that community. Getting that appointment was a reminder of how Nadeen and I were brought up. Our parents had encouraged us to trust in God to work things out. He knows what's best."

For the next nine years, Rock Island watched a postmaster who went far beyond his job requirements. They noticed how he showed special kindness to non-English speaking customers. He'd also re-wrap problem packages himself to ensure their safe arrival. He tried to attend community events even though he lived elsewhere. One time he helped raise money to buy new dentures for the community's retired minister, who lived on a very limited income.

Such positive character qualities didn't go unheralded. In 1992 Earl went before 2,500 applauding colleagues to receive the coveted "National Postmaster of the Year" award. Since then he has held two national postmaster association offices. He also moved to a larger, county-seat post office, again within driving distance of home.

Earl hasn't allowed such blessings to dim his conviction that he's ultimately working for the Lord. One time a national officer included off-color jokes in his speech to the state convention. Troubled, Earl wrote the national board expressing his personal disappointment over barroom humor. His gracious but forthright reaction caused a change at the national level.

Another time, as a candidate himself for national office, he was bothered by the presence of alcoholic drinks in candidates' campaign "hospitality rooms." Earl, a non-drinker, asked his church men's group to pray before he approached his committee about serving sparkling cider instead in his campaign room. "They passed my resolution in thirty seconds," Earl recalls. "I knew there were drinkers among them, so I asked if they were certain about their decision. They said that if people wanted alcoholic drinks, they could go to somebody else's room. What a wonderful answer to prayer this was."

The fires in Earl's life strengthened his conviction that God takes care of his own. He wants his life and work to glorify God, whatever the cost. Many years ago Earl and Nadeen decided their life focus was expressed by Joshua 24:15: "As for me and my household, we will serve the Lord." That biblical principle helped them obey God and ignore faithless and vindictive advice when testing fires came. They had their priorities right.

I don't know yet what God will bring from our family's accident and Grandma's cancer. It takes little effort to complain when life is hard. But my study about the fires at Taberah has made me more sensitive about how tendencies to complain are proportional to the distance we put between ourselves and God. Israel's complainers were on the outskirts of the camp. I wander there when I let life's busyness pull me into adopting the attitudes of people who live apart from God. Instead, I need to stay close to the heart of worship—in prayer, Bible reading, and the inner assurance that his hand is on my life.

Thus, instead of focusing on loss, I need to remember all that God has done for us. We have salvation in Jesus Christ. We have each other. God has always fed, clothed, and housed us, and filled our lives with pleasures and honors. When people ask about the accident, I am quick to say, "God spared us. It was an act of his grace."

Meanwhile, I am praying for the salvation of the man who wronged us! And through all of this, I am gaining, little by little, a deeper understanding of why fires refine.

Mileposts

1. What was God's major concern for the Israelites once they settled in the Promised Land? Check the clues in Deuteronomy 6:10-12; 8:11; and 32:18. How might that apply to you?
2. It's said that a man is known by the company he keeps. What does 2 Timothy 2:16-17a suggest might happen if you spend too much time with contentious people?
3. Another way to look at the problems of Numbers 11 is the Big Me. The Israelites were basically saying, "I come first. My needs, comforts, and wishes need priority attention." What is God's priority? See Isaiah 58:6-10 for one answer. Can you suggest another Scripture passage?
4. From Psalm 103, name things that are "forgotten" and "remembered."
5. Have you had a difficult experience that could be described as "walking through fire"? Memorize this for comfort: "When you walk through the fire, you will not be burned; the flames will not set you ablaze" (Isa. 43:2b).

Then they despised the pleasant land; they did not believe his promise. They grumbled in their tents.—Psalm 106:24-25

10
There Are Giants over There!

Pessimism and Certainty

We're one scary year away from our first child pressuring us for his driver's permit. It seems just yesterday this boy was safely strapped in his carseat with a plastic steering wheel and a red horn that went "beep beep." Now he's taller than his mother and shaves once a week. Whenever I drive him somewhere and a red blur passes us, he immediately intones the name, year, engine, and price tag of that blur.

I always have a good response: "What do you think that guy pays for car insurance?" Even his father's dire prediction of how our own insurance rates will zoom doesn't seem to faze him. He's growing up, and learning to drive is an important rite of passage.

I have a friend who survived teaching three teens to drive. His favorite practice course was the local cemetery. (I'll spare you the obvious jokes about that!) He told me that such a location provided lots of turns and stops—and not too many pedestrians. I know others who opted for our church parking lot—on days other than Sunday.

My dear parents risked life, limb, and fire hydrants to teach me to drive. I'll never forget my first drive down 13th

Street. One block and twenty feet before the semi-busy, residential Pioneer Avenue, my father shouted, "Turn right!" My reflexes not being quite what they should be, only his strong arm on the wheel prevented me from shearing off the fire plug at 13th and 1st. Disgusted, he turned over driving instruction to my mother, who actually dared to take me out on Pioneer. "I'm not good enough yet!" I whimpered as we waited ten minutes at the stop sign while every car within two miles went first. We might have waited there until bedtime, except my mother's patience finally wore thin.

Fear rides along on any great venture. Life's road may be winding, rough, and have its share of blind spots. But we'll get nowhere if we just pull off to the safety of the shoulder. The Hebrews' next stop shows us some vital truths about fear:

- Life will offer challenges to avoid or embrace.
- We need to guard our attitudes.
- We need to guard our choice of companions.
- We need to guard our mouths.

Challenges—to Avoid or Embrace

Fear leaves us two choices. We can anticipate failure or we can camp on success. To put it another way, we can be pessimists or optimists. Author James Branch Cabell once quipped in *The Silver Stallion*, "The optimist proclaims that we live in the best of all possible worlds; the pessimist fears this is true."[15] Or, to go back to the old glass-of-water definition, the optimist sees it half full rather than half empty. The optimist also drops in a few ice cubes and watches as nature's best liquid zooms right to the rim. Then there's the pessimist, analyzing the gloomy bottom half of the glass. Plus, he or she is despairing over water spots!

The Hebrews came to the border of Canaan eager to enter what they believed would be the best of all possible worlds. They'd waited a year for this moment, even though Egypt and Canaan were only eleven days apart by the Mount Seir road. But that road near the Mediterranean was also inhabited by hordes of people eager to turn the Hebrews into hamburger. Instead, God detoured them onto the scenic route, where they were able to develop the national identity and organization they'd need to claim their new home territory. This wouldn't be a tidy real-estate transaction, though; it meant blood.

Yielding to the people's anxiety, Moses sent twelve spies ahead. When they returned forty days later, staggering under a branch bearing a cluster of grapes, they filed contradictory reports. Ten were pessimists; two were optimists. Ten gave one positive observation: "It does flow with milk and honey" (Num. 13:27). And grapes! They then added with long faces: "But the people who live there are powerful, and the cities are fortified and very large. We even saw descendants of Anak there" (v. 28).

The truth was that they'd seen three unusually large men whose tribal name, Anak, literally means "sons of a necklace" or, possibly, "long-necked, tall men." We still have sons of Anak around. Just check out any basketball game. Or look out over a congregation and see who's so tall that nobody sits right behind! The ten trembling spies concluded that these slam-dunk types were all over the land. But the two optimists, Joshua and Caleb, urged the people to trust God: "We should go up and take possession of the land, for we can certainly do it" (v. 30). Ten trembled and two triumphed. Ten faced big giants; two faced a big God.

I remember the April day my 4 foot 7 inch twelve-year-old daughter described conquering the "giants" at Foothills Middle School. She was among those Foothills' sixth graders who were chosen to visit elementary school to assure petrified fifth graders that kids do live through their first year of middle school. But I remembered just a year before, when she sat nervously on the audience side of the assembly. Then summer passed and the first day of middle school loomed. Could she make it to classes on time? Could she remember both her hall and gym locker combinations? Could she survive harder math? spell harder words, like *icicle?* live through P.E. fitness days? Sure she could. And she did. Now we face the giants of high school and beyond!

I remember my giants from that era. As I faced college, my biggest concerns were investing my baby-sitting savings (at fifty cents an hour) in a manual typewriter, getting assigned a compatible roommate, and having enough intelligence to pass the seven-credit humanities course required of all freshmen. That last item alone was adequate reason for fear. We all stumbled out of the humanities midterm knowing we had met the enemy—and it was multiple choice and essay!

Bloomers and gloomers. Every family probably has at least one of each. But over the last couple of years we've acquired some new slogans about those plus-and-minus attitudes, thanks to a new friend named Dan Miller. If anyone had a reason to look at the dark side, Dan did.

Dan started his life journey at an enthusiastic sprint. At high school graduation in 1955, Dan was an all-American guy: a student body president with sports honors all over his letterman's jacket. He was captain of a league championship basketball team and named to an all-star team. He played on football teams that were undefeated for three consecutive years. He lettered in track and baseball. It's little wonder that he wanted to go to college and become a physical education teacher. He had other dreams too: to marry a great woman, have great kids, play guitar in his own band, and fly his own airplane.

A few weeks after graduation, he came home from driving a tractor on his folks' farm. He planned to shower and then jump in his '51 Ford in time for the movie in the next town. But he didn't feel that sharp. He thought he might be coming down with the flu. He was nauseated, feverish, and had a stiff neck. His mother was worried, and she had reason to be. Polio was killing and maiming people by the thousands. And while the Salk vaccine had just come out, it hadn't yet reached their small town of Pateros, Washington.

As Dan worsened, his family called the doctor. He found

no reflexes and confirmed that it was polio. They had two choices: rush Dan to a hospital sixty miles away or isolate him at home. They kept him home, secluded in his small bedroom in a corner of the basement. Friends could only visit by peering through a tiny, dirty window. Dan's mother, risking her own health, fed him and took care of other needs as paralysis eventually claimed his body. When his fever broke two weeks later, his body was so stiff he couldn't bend. Three people picked him up on their shoulders like a piece of timber and carried him out of the basement to a borrowed station wagon to go to the hospital. There, doctors determined that polio had destroyed eighty percent of the muscles in Dan's legs. His right arm was virtually useless. His left arm had only half its original muscle. One doctor predicted he'd be in a wheelchair for the rest of his life. This certainly wasn't how Dan had planned things.

Attitudes On Guard

We will always face "giants" in life. They might be personal goals in education or employment. They may be relationship problems, financial difficulties, or health setbacks. The critical test is how we deal with them. Numbers 13–14 shows how the Hebrews flunked this next test. Even though God had done so much for them already, they refused to believe he would provide anything better. Just listen to them whine:

> All the Israelites grumbled against Moses and Aaron, and the whole assembly said to them, "If only we had died in Egypt! Or in this desert! Why is the Lord bringing us to this land only to let us fall by the sword? Our wives and children will be taken as plunder. Wouldn't it be better for us to go back to Egypt?" (Numbers 14:2-3)

You can't get much more pessimistic than that! There's a vital clue to their grumbling in the original Hebrew. The verb for "grumbled" *(lun)* expressed resentment, dissatisfaction, anger, and hostile, dark murmuring. (Sounds a bit like professional sports!) Remember, the Hebrews had already grumbled over water and manna. Each time they grumbled, they ignored God's protection, provision, and plan. They insulted his justice, goodness, and power. God said their refusal to believe his Word and miracles was the same as treating him with contempt (Num. 14:11). How could he continue to support and help them when they were rejecting him?

Similarly, how often does God bring us to a place where we can have great victories or do great things in his name, and we plop down and whine about it instead? We say, "God, it's too hard," or "God, I'll never make it." But God didn't design us to doubt his ability to work things out. He wants us to press assuredly ahead, willing to take him at his word.

Guarding our attitudes means going into each day expecting God's best. Psalm 5:3 says, "In the morning I lay my requests before you and wait in expectation." I love to get up and eat breakfast before the family, watching the sun rise. My son sometimes does that, too. I'll come in the kitchen and see him with his chin on the windowsill, watching the sky ignite with pinks and oranges, his bowl of cereal hardly touched. It's a reminder that every day is a new opportunity from God. It also reminds us that there will be something positive in every situation, even if we have to throw up our hands and cry out, "I don't understand!" If we can still affirm that God is on the throne, then we're acknowledging his power and authority. How I love the hope of Habakkuk 3:17-18. Even when invading nations had destroyed crops and livestock, Habakkuk could hang on to the big "yet": *"Yet* I will rejoice in the Lord, I will be joyful in God my Savior." There may be giants about, *yet* my God is bigger than they are.

Dan Miller's "giants" haunted the hospital rehabilitation room where aides wheeled his paralyzed body. Giving up and withering away would have been easy. But Dan tackled the challenge, hopeful for what rehab could do for him. It wasn't fun by any stretch of the imagination. He'd scream in pain as therapists bent his limbs to tear away dead muscle and build up what was left. He'd scream the loudest the days one particular therapist, Carmen, worked on him; she had a hearing loss and kindly turned off her hearing aid!

Dan tried to look for the positive in his situation. He injected his sense of humor into the gloomy sameness of hospital life, talking his friends into pushing his wheelchair into the hospital's secret corners or playing tricks on nurses (like pouring strong perfume into bedpans).

He also reached back to a faith nurtured in childhood. At eleven, he'd prayed at the altar of his folks' little church to become a Christian. He grew up hearing people pray, and he knew that his family's and friends' prayers had kept him from total paralysis, even death. Now the prayer goal was recovery. "I asked God to let me regain enough muscle strength to be independent," Dan remembers. "It was so humbling to have somebody else feed me, dress me, bathe me, and lift me onto a toilet." He wanted so much to walk, that one day, ignoring doctor's orders, he slid off the side of his bed, locked his legs, attempted a step, and promptly collapsed. Unable to reach a call button, he lay there a long time before he was discovered and reprimanded. But he never gave up.

Recovery came literally one finger at a time. Therapists had rigged some elastic tubing above his bed to exercise his good arm. However, he often lost his grip and couldn't lift the arm back up to the tubing. Then he realized he could crab-walk his fingers up his body, dragging the nearly dead arm along. When his hand reached his head and dropped forward, it went right to the tubing. "It wasn't very much," Dan says, "but it was my first success in overcoming the polio and being able to do something by myself."

Choosing Our Companions Wisely

A hundred days after entering the hospital horizontally, Dan hobbled out vertically, a forearm crutch gripped in his half-good left arm. He went home to another year of therapy on contraptions set up in his parents' kitchen. And he fought more giants who sneered, "You'll never be the same again." As he began to dream again of attending college, he found encouragement the most important therapy.

All of us need Calebs and Joshuas in our lives, people who can look beyond initial impressions and see God's hand at work. We need to heed the Bible when it tells us that "bad company corrupts good character" (1 Cor. 15:33) and that we should "walk in the ways of good men and keep to the paths of the righteous" (Prov. 2:20). Our closest friends should help us, instruct us, and lift us up.

Dan Miller calls such people "dream makers." Fifteen months after polio, he hobbled onto a college campus to register for classes. Clutching a registration packet stamped "P. E. Exempt," he fell six times on his way to the college field house to see his adviser, one of the P.E. professors. As he sat down and dropped his crutch, Dan laid out his fragile dreams.

"I can't do push-ups or pull-ups, climb stairs, or jump rope," he told his adviser. "But I still want to major in physical education." He expected the man to suggest Dan find another major. Instead, the adviser just smiled and said, "Let's see what you can do." Those six words made the difference. Dan went on to eventually earn his master's degree and certification to teach both elementary and secondary physical education. He landed a P. E. job over able-bodied candidates, overcoming the limitations of his disability with a positive outlook and creative zest.

Teaching wasn't the only dream Dan refused to abandon when polio changed his life. In college he invented a new way to strum the guitar by resting his useless right thumb on the guitar neck. Then he put together a band whose engagements helped pay college expenses—and which also won a regional "battle of the bands" and made a recording. And he met Judy, winning her heart from a fullback who played for the University of Washington. One day that boyfriend came to visit and, learning of her interest in Dan, remarked, "That guy's a cripple!"

Judy retorted, "He's not a cripple when you get to know him!" Dan and Judy married and became parents of three children. With Judy as his cheerleader, he dared to challenge some other barriers, including golfing one-armed (he's scored 38—6 pars—on nine holes) and getting his pilot's license (proving wrong the people who predicted he'd decorate a hill with a Cessna).

Guarding Our Mouths

The three most dangerous phrases in the English language are these: "What if—," "I can't—," and "Yes, but—." Those *ifs*, *can'ts* and *buts* only reinforce our tendency to give up. Of course, there's a proper place for caution and for seeking godly counsel. But we'll never progress if we continue to throw excuses in the path of hope. We'll copy the infamous sluggard in Proverbs 22:13 who avoided work by crying out, without evidence, "There is a lion outside!" or "I will be murdered in the streets!" Remember the verbal guidelines of Ephesians 4:29: "Do not let any unwholesome talk come out of your mouths, but only what is helpful for building others up according to their needs, that it may benefit those who listen."

Dan has long practiced positive communication. When he moved from teaching into elementary administration, he became known throughout the state for his positive, fun approach to leadership. Three state education awards came his way. A major television station even featured one positive project, his *Good Kids Book*.

At Leavenworth, Washington, he started a program in which children with good behavior were sent to the principal's office for positive reinforcement. Any adult staff or faculty member could send a child to Dan for commendable behaviors ranging from showing kindness to finishing a hard task. The kids would sign Dan's *Good Kids Book* and munch

143

on snacks while he called a parent at work or home to brag about them.

"Even if a parent was in a meeting at work, I'd always get through," Dan says. "Parents want to hear good things about their children."

Dan's campaign to slay the giant of school humdrum included wearing goofy hats, bedroom slippers, funny buttons, and silly ties. He patrolled the playground on his trail bike and rode it into opening assemblies. He'd play his guitar for all-school sing-alongs. Kids loved the unpredictability.

But probably his "I Love Monday" campaign hit the most tender nerve of pessimism.

"A lot of people seemed to believe that old saying, 'On Mondays, I rise and whine,'" Dan observed. He told his faculty that all future Mondays would get special treatment. After all, they were one-fifth of the work week. He flooded the school with signs about Mondays: "I Love Monday," "I Live for Monday," and "TGIM" (Thank God It's Monday!). On Fridays, he'd declare, "Only two and a half days until Monday!" The positive messages caught on. A few years later, when Dan retired from education and began a career as a speaker, his "I Love Monday" signs became his trademark. He even changed his telephone number so the last four digits would read *TGIM*.

So far, more than a quarter of a million people have heard Dan tell about his "I Love Monday" campaign. They've also met a man who faced the giant called polio but refused to let it define his life. He urges audiences to appropriate the six words he got from his college adviser: "Let's see what you can do."

"We can either be dream makers or dream breakers," Dan tells both business and Christian audiences as he encourages them to face the giants in their own lives. A big part of his message is that people need to laugh more—and he helps his audience do that with silly hats, slides, and one-liners. Dan uses his paralysis as the bridge to deliver life principles to people experiencing emotional and spiritual paralysis. He's an overcomer, but underneath it all is a deep conviction that we best face our giants with the Lord alongside.

"Over and over, I've seen in my life the truth of Ephesians 3:20," says Dan. "That verse says God is able to do 'immeasurably more than all we ask or imagine, according to his power that is at work within us.' I know that's true of every physical gain I've made since polio. I know it describes the blessings God has poured out on my profession and ministry."

Before Dan speaks anywhere, he always walks through the room or auditorium to pray for his presentation and the people coming. He knows many face giants in their jobs or families. Some, like him, deal with giants in their own bodies. One time after speaking he was approached by a man who'd been hit by a drunk driver the previous year. The man suffered paralysis plus a head injury that impaired his speech, vision, and thinking. Doctors had written him off as hopeless, but the man had heard Dan speak just three months before the accident.

"As this man told me his story, he shared how four words from my speech—'You can do it'—kept him going through recovery," Dan remembers. "I was overjoyed to see him and realize how God used me."

People often pair *pessimism* and *optimism* as opposites. But there's another word that's a better antithesis for the attitude that looks at life darkly. It's *certainty*. Optimism hopes for the best possible outcome. Certainty moves beyond hope to affirm that the best is yet to come. That's Dan Miller's message, and it's also the one God gives through the life of Caleb, one of the two spies who dared to return excited about the new homeland. "We should go up and take possession of the land," he said, "for we can *certainly* do it" (Num. 13:30, emphasis mine). Or, to paraphrase Dan's college adviser, "Let's see what you and God can do." We know the attitude God prefers: "Because my servant Caleb has a different spirit and follows me wholeheartedly, I will bring him into the land he went to, and his descendants will inherit it" (Num. 14:24).

Only Caleb and Joshua set foot in the Promised Land from that generation. All the other Hebrews who originally came from slavery in Egypt—all the grumblers—would eventually perish in the wilderness.

But habits of grumbling die hard. The incident with the spies could be compared with what Winston Churchill said at a critical turn of World War II: "This is not the end. It is not even the beginning of the end. But it is, perhaps, the end of the beginning." In the next chapter we'll come to a grumbling incident that finally represents "the beginning of the end."

Mileposts

1. What are your Mondays like? Do you drag through the week until you get to Friday, then limp through the whole week cycle again? What would it take to turn the tide of negativism where you work or live? Write "TGIM" on a 3 x 5 card and put it at your work place or on your bathroom mirror.
2. Read Hebrews 3:12-19, then go back and underline verse 14. What does it mean to "hold firmly till the end the confidence we had at first"? Describe that for the Hebrews and then for your own life.
3. Sometimes we get our hardest lessons from the consequences of negativism. What insight do you get from Isaiah 29:24? Read Numbers 14:39-45. What was the main reason for their defeat?
4. We don't hear about Caleb again until he enters the Promised Land at the age of eighty-five. Read Joshua 14:6-15. Had his enthusiasm ebbed with age? For fun, compare Joshua 15:14 with Numbers 13:22.
5. Memorize Dan Miller's favorite verse: "Now to him who is able to do immeasurably more than all we ask or imagine, according to his power that is at work within us" (Eph. 3:20).

They turned their backs to me and not their faces.—Jeremiah 32:33

11
I'll Do It <u>My</u> Way

Pride and Submission

What would manufacturers of sport utility vehicles do without TV ads showing their vehicles going where none has dared to go before? Hills that go nearly straight up? No problem. Mud up to your armpits? Bring it on! A trail furnished with boulders the size of a grizzly bear? Just watch the steering on this baby. The folks who write and film those ads know how to appeal to our secret craving to draw our own maps.

We learn it early. When both my kids were preschoolers, Inga loved to play house. "You be the daddy and I'll be the mommy," I'd hear her order her brother, Zach. "We'll go shopping and then clean the house." However, Zach had already mapped out his day, something on the order of "you do your thing with your dollies and I'll do my things with my Legos." It didn't improve much as they grew older. They acquired some soccer skills, and our front yard (with its fourteen vulnerable rose bushes) became their playing field—until their two sets of rules clashed and one child stomped into the house.

Then they learned to read and entered the wonderful world of board games. Who reads all the fine print on the inside of the Monopoly box? One does—to prove wrong the one who doesn't. Pride ends the game before anybody even has a chance to buy Boardwalk.

Then they become teenagers. "Why make beds when you just climb back in at night?" "I don't want to wear a coat—it's only a little blizzard outside." "Nobody else goes to bed before the sun sets!" I'm told we do survive, but pride and rebellion are powerful distractions. We want to do things our own way, and we chafe at authority.

There are two kinds of pride. One can be proud of an honorable achievement or relationship. I'm fiercely proud of my children and their accomplishments. I often tell them, "I'm so proud you're my son," or "It's sure great having you for a daughter." But there's also arrogant pride, which is offensive to God. It writes its own moral code in defiance of God's principles for living. We see it in leaders who defend immoral behavior as "expedient." We experience it in our homes and offices when the quest for power and advantage drives wedges in relationships.

Arrogant pride goes back to the very heart of our relationship with God. When we declare, "I'll do life my way," we are telling God that we want to build our own system of faith. But God will judge such arrogance. The wilderness journey included two religious rebellions that, sadly, illustrate such choices:

- Pride rejects God's roadmap.
- Pride draws its own map.
- Pride's map leads others astray.
- Pride's detours cost dearly.
- Broken pride restores blessing.

Who Needs a Map?

Whenever my family traveled somewhere, my dad found it difficult to admit he was lost until he had nearly driven the family to Antarctica. It was too hard on his ego to yield to

Mother's plea, "Please stop in at some nice service station and ask." After all, didn't God create men with that extra sense that could almost smell the way to a destination? (The answer is no—unless you're headed for the fast-food district or a pig farm.)

People often show the same arrogance regarding the things of God. They think they can "wing it" and disregard God's map, the Bible. They quote wonderful, phony verses like "God helps those who help themselves" and "Cleanliness is next to godliness." They think that's enough to stake their lives on.

Such attitudes mirror the error of Aaron's sons Nadab and Abihu in Leviticus 10. God had just given his people the Law and officially inaugurated the work of the priesthood. He gave very specific instructions for worship, including burning incense. But Nadab and Abihu refused to follow the rules. They "took their censers, put fire in them and added incense; and they offered unauthorized fire before the Lord, contrary to his command" (Lev. 10:1). What is _unauthorized fire?_ Most likely it was fire that didn't originate from the brazen altar, which God had ignited supernaturally (Lev. 9:24). God was very protective of this fire and had commanded priests to never let it go out (Lev. 6:12-13). God judged their disobedience instantly, incinerating them with his presence.

Was God arbitrary and harsh? No. He had to impress on a people softened by the influence of idolatry that he was an absolutely holy God: "Among those who approach me I will show myself holy; in the sight of all the people I will be honored" (Lev. 10:3).

Hilton and Lorna Jarvis have taken that command seriously and tried to pass it on to their three children. But one, Gregg, chose his own way.

I first met Gregg when I was in my early twenties and he was about six. I'd moved to his town with my first job and started attending the church his father pastored. Single, new in my faith, and very lonely, I gravitated toward his bubbly, caring mother. She often included me in family meals, helped me laugh, and shared valuable counsel.

I enjoyed being an "auntie" to the Jarvis kids. How can I forget doing surgery on their leaking beanbag frog? Delivering by bike hot bread I'd just made from scratch? Having them all to spaghetti dinner in my six-by-six dinette? Playing with their "wiener dog"? Or just plopping on the sofa in the TV room to watch *Gilligan's Island?* Sandwiched between a do-all bigger brother and a cute-beyond-words baby sister, Gregg was a fun kid who had a hard time obeying. He was ten when I left town.

In the years before I saw him again, I knew his parents struggled with him. Though they'd tried to raise all three children by the same standards, Gregg was their challenge— a free spirit, strong willed, and apt to risk punishment.

He also had a sensitive spirit, wounded when the youth pastor he admired was forced to resign. He experienced other hurts connected to church life. When a church family sold him a van when he was a just-licensed sixteen year old, other church teens implied he'd use the van for immoral purposes. Another time, while waiting in line with a friend at a multi-show movie theater, some teens from his church wrongly accused him of going to an X-rated film. "He got so frustrated over those incidents," recalled his father. "He told us, 'If this is the way people in the church are, I'm not sure I want to be a part of it.' "

He had a girlfriend whose father was a church leader. "Their relationship was very special," his mother said. "It was devastating when they broke up. Worse, many unkind things were said about Gregg, and he became more disillusioned with Christians. When he was a senior, we allowed him to attend another Bible-teaching church to help him get a fresh start. We don't know how often he went, though he did bring home a bulletin a few times."

When I saw him again a decade later, Gregg still had that you've-gotta-be-kidding smile and kid-brother sense of humor. But something was different.

Pride Draws Its Own Map

Pride tries to come up with its own way to God. In the summer of 1996, between his criminal and civil murder trials, O. J. Simpson turned up at a Los Angeles church to become an "honorary member." He told them he wasn't trying to restore his image or regain his wealth. "I'm trying to do one thing," he said. "I'm trying to go to heaven."[16]

That sounds like a commendable goal. But spiritual pride always "tries" to get to heaven. Behind those pious words is the implication that we can come up with our own way to God. Some people attend churches that deny Jesus died for our sins to provide a way to heaven. They believe that Jesus was a great teacher, but he was not the Son of God. They hope that a good life will assure them some sort of reward after they die. How wrong they are! We approach God only through Jesus Christ. "No one comes to the Father except through me," he said in John 14:6.

A lot of people stumble here. The cross is too awful and too hard to understand: Why would a loving God allow a good man to be killed in such a torturous way?

Years ago, shortly after I asked Christ into my life, I visited a couple who attended a church that stressed moral living more than Christ's role in reconciliation with God. One time I sat down at their piano and opened a hymnal to "The Old Rugged Cross." As I started playing, the wife came out of the kitchen and said, "Please play another, that one's so bloody!" As a young Christian I was taken aback by her reaction—and I missed an opportunity to affirm how that bloodied cross made a difference for me! Very simply, people don't like the cross: "For the message of the cross is foolishness to those who are perishing, but to us who are being saved it is the power of God" (1 Cor. 1:18).

Gregg knew about the cross. As a preacher's kid, he'd heard lots of altar calls. He had several Bibles. But none of it put his life in focus. After high school, Gregg found jobs here and there. He picked up a different set of friends. At 19 he moved out, leaving behind some trash bags for his parents to put out for the garbage truck. Inside one was a Bible.

"I retrieved it and kept it," said his father. "I'm glad I did. Over the years I read through passages Gregg had underlined and starred. I read the notes he made in the margins. They showed me that at one time in his life Gregg understood God's desires and expectations of him." Two underlined passages especially stood out as Hilton wrestled with his son's rebellion:

> In my mind I want to be God's willing servant but instead I find myself still enslaved to sin. So you see how it is: my new life tells me to do right, but the old nature that is still inside me loves to sin. Oh, what a terrible predicament I'm in! Who will free me from my slavery to this deadly lower nature? Thank God! It has been done by Jesus Christ our Lord. He has set me free. (Romans 7:24-25, TLB)

> Don't be misled; remember that you can't ignore God and get away with it: a man will always reap just the kind of crop he sows! (Galatians 6:7, TLB)

Pride's Map Misleads

In middle school, my son, Zach, showed promise as a cartographer, thanks to a seventh-grade teacher whose personal interest in world travel translated into stressing map drawing for social studies. Zach spent hours poring over atlases, making sure each bay and mountain on his map was exactly where it should be. When the school year ended, he was drawing maps of imaginary worlds!

Fantasy maps are fine—where would we be if C. S. Lewis had never thought of Narnia?—but God has no patience for those who draw new spiritual maps. That's what happened in the second wilderness rebellion, described in Numbers 16. A tribal leader named Korah talked more than 250 others into protesting the fact that only those in Aaron's family could be priests. What probably brought the complaint to a head was an instruction at the end of chapter 15. God told the people to attach blue-threaded tassels to the corners of their clothes to remind them that they were God's holy people. Korah and his followers concluded that if the tassels represented the setting apart of all Israelites for holiness, then Aaron and his family didn't deserve preferential treatment.

On the surface, Korah's complaint sounds valid. But Korah failed to acknowledge that God set up the priesthood. God had designated the Kohathite branch of the Levites (which included Korah) for the number-two job of carrying the most sacred temple objects, including the ark (see Numbers 4:1-20). But Korah was a proud and grasping man who wanted to be Number One, a priest involved in sacrifices, just like his cousin. He wanted to draw his own map, reordering God's plan of relationships.

Gregg's rebellion also involved choosing relationships contrary to God's Word. A family friend of whom Gregg was very fond shared with Gregg's parents a letter in which Gregg talked bluntly about homosexual feelings. Hilton and Lorna never told Gregg what they'd read, but the letter confirmed what they'd observed.

Gregg left that relationship but got involved in another with a male ballet dancer. During that time, he called his mother and started talking about how he liked guys more than girls.

"Mom," he said, "I have a new family here."

"Gregg," she replied, "we're your family and we always will be, no matter what. You may feel this way now, but remember we always will be your family."

Gregg's rebellion continued. He moved in with yet another homosexual, "Dwayne," who'd be his partner for the next seven years.

Pride's Detours Cost Us

I'm usually the official map reader when we go on trips. I

don't mind, now that I have bifocals and can make out the mini labels. Being visually oriented helps, too. I remember my mother with her vision problems attempting to read the map for Dad as road signs zipped by at fifty bumpy miles an hour. I always wondered if their marriage would survive vacations, though we got some nice side excursions out of it!

The side trips weren't as pleasant for Korah's supporters. To straighten things out, Moses summoned Korah's supporters Dathan and Abiram. But they were so angry and alienated they refused to see him. They also dragged other issues into the conflict. They claimed Moses failed to deliver on his promise to take them to the Promised Land. They even called Egypt by Canaan's title, the "land flowing with milk and honey" (Num. 16:13), forgetting the misery of their enslavement in Egypt. Pride had so blinded them that they forgot how Moses had brought them to the edge of Canaan at Kadesh Barnea, but ten pessimistic spies turned their hearts.

Moses offered Korah and his followers another opportunity to set things right before God. But still the rebels stood in opposition. And again judgment came swiftly and thoroughly: the rebels were swallowed alive in a tremendous earthquake. There's another detail here that reveals the high price of pride; verses 27-33 tell us their wives and children died with them.

Families still pay a high personal price for rebellion. Gregg's decision favoring homosexuality tore at his parents' hearts. They faced hard choices in how they'd react, especially knowing how many of the men in Gregg's new "family" had been cut off by their real families.

"Lorna and I decided that we would not confront Gregg in this area," Hilton says. "We grieved over his choice of the sin of homosexuality. But we were going to love our son and love his friends unconditionally, as God does." As a result, Gregg and Dwayne were frequently in Lorna and Hilton's home, celebrating holidays and birthdays. Sometimes they'd drop in for no reason at all. "Gregg knew how we felt about his lifestyle," Hilton said. "He knew in his heart it went against what God said. But we kept the communication lines open. We just loved them in the Lord."

"We couldn't have loved them otherwise," added Lorna. "I was never crazy about Gregg's partner. But I knew I had to accept him if I wanted a relationship with my son." Though the relationship remained cordial, it was never very deep.

"Gregg and Dwayne had their expensive toys—their vehicles, fancy clothes, and electronics gear," Hilton remembered. "But these things only covered up their emptiness. We never pushed them to talk about spiritual things, but we also didn't change our lifestyle. We continued to pray at meals and read Scripture as part of our Christmas traditions. Dwayne listened respectfully but there was no warmth or openness."

As Lorna and Hilton wrestled with why homosexuality had touched their family, they honored Gregg's desire for privacy. Only his brother, his brother's wife, and his sister knew. "Gregg was very protective of us," Hilton said. "He'd watched us weather turmoil in other pastorates. He didn't want this church to reject us because of him."

But the ache of Gregg's rebellion continued. In late February 1992, during one of his morning walk-and-pray times, Hilton cried out to the Lord. "Oh, God," he said, "we've been praying for so many years. There's no indication at all that Gregg is open to you or interested in coming back to you. Lord, whatever it takes to bring Gregg back, we'll accept it." Hilton thought that a crisis with another family member might draw Gregg back into the faith. "But the Lord knew better," Hilton said. "That would only have made Gregg more bitter. Instead, God allowed affliction to land right on Gregg."

Two months after Hilton's prayer, Dwayne broke up with Gregg. Later, Gregg showed up at his parents' home looking thin and weary.

"As he left, he grabbed his mother and just hugged her," Hilton recalled. "He said, 'I know I look thin, but I haven't been able to eat, what with this break-up.' I saw him fight tears. He knew—though he didn't tell us at that time—that he was HIV positive and beginning to get AIDS."

In June, his parents paid his way to his sister's wedding in California. He wasn't well and Lorna remembers telling the Lord, "My daughter is gaining a new life and I fear my son is going to lose his."

His health deteriorated considerably over the next half year. In February 1993, Gregg checked himself into a hospital. His parents rushed up to Seattle to find him close to death. He admitted to them that he had full-blown AIDS, and he finally allowed them to tell their church. In telling Gregg's story to his church's leaders, Hilton offered to resign the pastorate he'd held for thirteen years. He thought that might be necessary if the elders felt he was not in control of his own home—the principle for leaders set forth in the New Testament. No one called for his resignation.

The next Sunday he stood before his congregation to read a letter explaining Gregg's circumstances and their hope of seeing him come back to the Lord before he died. Around him stood the church elders and his family. Afterward, the entire congregation came up in a show of love.

"We were overwhelmed by the church's support," Hilton said. "We never heard anything derogatory said. And now we had their prayer support as we went into the most difficult phase of Gregg's dying."

Gregg had resigned his job and gone on disability. Hilton and Lorna began what would be ten months of driving to see him every Saturday.

The Blessing of Broken Pride

Proverbs 11:2 says, "When pride comes, then comes disgrace, but with humility comes wisdom." God didn't want the people to forget the Korahite rebellion, so he had the mangled bronze of the dead men's censers hammered immediately onto the altar. But the Hebrews were so entrenched in pride and sin, the next day they again lashed out at Moses and Aaron. Again there was a price paid as a plague wiped out 14,700 people.

Why was the Korahite pride judged so severely? So that God could indelibly impress the necessity of submitting to him so that he could extend blessing to his chosen people.

This need to submit to God is illustrated in two ways in Gregg's story. One is how he chose his own way and was finally broken to submit to God. The other is how his parents' faith was refined by deeper submission to God in a ministry they never anticipated. Psalm 76:10 says even the wrath of men can bring God praise. This came true as AIDS took its toll on Gregg's body.

Hilton and Lorna's weekly visits opened their eyes to a whole culture of men who exist within their own network. Most revealed only their first name. Gregg had his own gay doctor, gay lawyer, and gay hairdresser.

"We met some fine young men," Lorna said. "They hold good jobs, pay their rent, keep their places clean, and most are not alcoholics or drug addicts. But they're blinded by their own prejudices about sexuality."

Gregg also had a baffling relationship with a female friend, "Jennifer," who joined him daily for lunch to watch a favorite soap opera. Though he'd turned away from God, Gregg still told Jennifer about knowing Jesus Christ. He even loaned her his Bible. She read it, went to church, and eventually became a fervent Christian. Jennifer had cared about Gregg enough at one point earlier to want to marry him, but he backed away, knowing by then he was HIV-positive.

Despite deteriorating health, Gregg declined his parents' request that he come home. Instead, he asked his former partner, Dwayne, to move back in and care for him. This was hard for Lorna, whose mothering instinct was strong. "Mothers take care of their children," she says. "Dwayne had done so much harm in Gregg's life, and I had to forgive him for coming back into it. I had to accept that Gregg's protective love for me meant he would die away from home."

She struggled, too, with why all this turmoil with Gregg had occupied their lives when they also had two other grown children and the demands of their church ministry. She remembers sitting at a stoplight one morning on the way to work and thinking, "God must love me a lot to have trusted me with this."

By November, Gregg wanted to plan his funeral. He told his parents the pain had become so bad that he'd been asking God to just let him go to sleep. Yet he was worried about whether Christians really went immediately to heaven. It was the spiritual opening his parents had prayed for.

"Gregg told me that although he'd accepted Christ as a boy," Hilton remembers, "he now wondered if God really wanted him in light of what he'd done with his life. I was able to share with him that if we truly confess our sins, God will forgive and cleanse us. He told me he'd asked God's forgiveness many times, and I could sense an earnestness in his face and voice. We talked again about how salvation was based on accepting what Christ had done."

A few weeks later, at only twenty-nine, Gregg died. People from Hilton's church and Lorna's office packed a funeral home for his service. Though none of Gregg's gay friends came to the funeral, a handful kept in touch with Lorna and Hilton, having learned to trust them through Gregg's illness.

"We knew we wouldn't reach them for Christ the usual way, by preaching the gospel," Lorna said. "We had to love them and wait for that moment of openness, even if it came through the reality of death."

That's what happened with Dwayne. Several weeks after Gregg's death, Dwayne and Jennifer joined Hilton and Lorna at a restaurant for dinner. "I've been reading this," Dwayne said, holding out Gregg's Bible.

"Why don't you keep it?" Hilton replied, going on to explain how to get the most out of reading the Bible. He knew that Jennifer, now a vibrant Christian, could also help.

Several months later, Dwayne was dying of AIDS in a nursing home. When Hilton visited him, Dwayne was ready to ask God's forgiveness and accept the gift of eternal life. When Dwayne died, Hilton, an evangelical Protestant pastor, was invited to share at the Catholic funeral alongside the priest who works full-time with AIDS patients and their families. As Hilton read Scripture and spoke, he noticed one of Gregg's friends, an AIDS patient on an experimental treatment, weeping uncontrollably. Knowing his own death was close, he wanted to meet with Hilton later.

"God really challenged us to depend on him to love Gregg and his friends," Hilton says. "We still grieve over the sin of homosexuality, but God used this to show us how to love homosexuals unconditionally, as he does. I also learned that God is sovereign in how he uses circumstances to accomplish what is needed to bring someone back. For Gregg, it took AIDS. If he hadn't gotten AIDS, he probably would have continued in that lifestyle, thumbing his nose at God. But it forced him to face his life and his relationship with God. I miss my son very much, but I'm grateful I'll see him again in heaven."

When I prayed for the Jarvises through this trial, I sometimes asked God why their family should experience such sorrow. They've always tried to honor God. Both the other children have established Christian homes, and their new son-in-law is a pastor. Sometimes we don't understand why choices by family members should pull us over such rutted roads. This side of heaven, we won't get satisfactory answers—only God's road map to take us where he knows we should go.

What about times we stumble on the trail alone? The next chapter gives a whole new meaning to the expression "serpentine routes."

Mileposts

1. What might be a point of rebellion in your life? Is there a moral issue? Or one concerning your parents' or employer's authority? Is there bondage to money or success or popularity? Evaluate it in light of Romans 7:15-25.
2. Read Romans 6:13 and determine how its message confirms the principles given in this chapter.

3. What sins are singled out in 1 Corinthians 6:9-10 and Colossians 3:5-9? Which involve the body? the mind? Which might touch on your weaknesses? What does Colossians 3:10-17 suggest for dealing with those sinful desires?

4. What does 2 Corinthians 4:1-6 say about sharing Christ with those in bondage or rebellion?

5. In our distress over the consequences of rebellion, it's easy to forget the promises that follow repentance and submission. Memorize "the rest of the story": "You were washed, you were sanctified, you were justified in the name of the Lord Jesus Christ and by the Spirit of our God" (1 Cor. 6:11).

The steps of the godly are directed by the LORD.
He delights in every detail of their lives.
Though they stumble, they will not fall,
for the LORD holds them by the hand.—*Psalm 37:23,* NLT

12
Why Me?

Grumbling and Reconciliation

My first car was known for running up extraordinary bills for mechanical transplants at the local car hospital. My checkbook bled every time my car leaked vital fluids, screeched when I braked, or shivered and coughed when I turned off the ignition. When I sold the car after a hundred-thousand-and-something feeble miles, I wished I could have added all my repair expenses to the price! The bottom line would have bought a mighty ritzy replacement.

Over a lifetime, we'll buy and "bye" a number of cars. But we don't have that option with our bodies. We get one. That's it. I know that's a disappointing fact for many teenagers, who'd do anything to trade their pimples, bad hair, and big feet for improved models. It won't happen. God calls us to take care of what we've got.

That mandate has enabled our family to keep several doctors, dentists, and orthodontists in fancy wheels. Besides supporting the automobile industry with their bodies, my children have provided me with a fairly complete medical education.

My firstborn entered the world without apparent problems, a healthy eight-pounder fattened by my pregnancy cravings for roasted peanuts. We weathered the usual colds and ear infections, until they just started getting worse. His besieged tonsils hung in his throat like warty lima beans, luring every germ within sneezing range. At five, he and his tonsils parted ways. Then one morning he woke up in great pain with what looked like one-sided mumps. Diagnosis: an infected salivary gland. After four or so encore performances by that infection over several years—and the semi-annual siege of allergies to everything that bloomed or shed fur or feathers—I hoped the end was in sight.

Then one hot evening he went for a ride on his bike and turned from passenger to human cannonball. His helmet saved his brain, but he snapped his collar bone—just a couple heartbreaking days before a summer job watching a neighbor's house with a swimming pool (with permission to use the pool anytime a parent was present). Arm in sling, he woefully paced in the shallow end, dreaming of the dives that wouldn't be.

Then his dentist handed us the next verdict: braces.

"Why me?" Zach whined, as we visited the orthodontist and prepared for the installation of oral barbed-wire fencing. "Why does everything have to go wrong with *my* body?" I hugged him and promised him I'd make his sandwiches with soft white bread.

More bike tumbles, insect bites, and nasty falls followed the next summer. We went through several boxes of adhesive bandages. Despite Mom's warnings to "not scratch," he did.

When he complained of a hot, hard place on his leg, I rushed him to the doctor, who got concerned about possible blood poisoning. "Why me?" he whined, as I kept him home a day from school to monitor him and keep the antibiotics going.

Back to the dentist. This time his twelve-year molars emerged with ready-made cavities. "A congenital defect," said the dentist. "Why me?" my son moaned again.

We all have our medical stories, some more than their share! Every one of us, at some time or other, has wanted to grumble, "Why me?" It's an old, old song, memorably sung in Numbers 21 with several vital principles for living:

- Grumbling results when expectations exceed needs.
- God knows how much we can handle.
- Lifting up Jesus Christ puts down grumbling.
- The weaker we get, the stronger God works.

Expectations Versus Needs

Numbers 21 is like the week before graduation. You've slugged through the tests and papers, you've got spring fever, and you can hardly wait to get it over with.

After forty years of going in circles, the Hebrews saw the end in sight. They'd won battles over old enemies. First, they turned back the Canaanites of Arad. Victory was especially sweet since it came at a town called Hormah, the same place they met defeat thirty-eight years earlier when they tried to enter Canaan on their own (Num. 14:45).

After the battle at Hormah, they had to backtrack to go around Edom before entering the Promised Land. That meant going back to the desert, back to the Red Sea road, and then a broad swing to the east. They were so close, and yet so far, from finishing their years of wandering.

> But the people grew impatient on the way; they spoke against God and against Moses, and said, "Why have you brought us up out of Egypt to die in the desert? There is no bread! There is no water! And we detest this miserable food!" (Numbers 21:4b-5)

Of course, God had provided food and water. It wasn't steak, baked potatoes with sour cream and chives, and freshly steamed broccoli, served with a tall glass of lemon water, but God still provided rations. Yet they complained. Their problem was that their expectations exceeded their needs.

Sometimes I'm apt to forget all that God has done and is doing, and I slip into old habits of grumbling and wishing things were different. I allow discontent to stir in my heart and then exit my mouth in complaints that do nobody any good. Psalm 140:3 comes too close for comfort: "They make their tongues as sharp as a serpent's; the poison of vipers is on their lips." The same for James 3:8: "[The tongue] is a restless evil, full of deadly poison."

No wonder God sent, as punishment, poisonous snakes: "Then the Lord sent venomous snakes among them; they bit the people and many Israelites died" (Num. 21:6). The snakes might have been a native cobra whose bite is very deadly.

Rattlesnakes inhabit the hills above our home; I have no desire to invite them to my picnics. My fear of snakes helps me imagine the Hebrews' horror as thousands of deadly serpents invaded their camp. Today, we're not as apt to find snakes knocking at our front doors. But we may experience similar dismay when our bodies are attacked by other strange and painful things.

Pastor Harlan Humiston knows about that. At thirty-nine, having always had good health, he was enjoying his work in the church along with Linda, his wife, and his busy family of five children. About the time they moved into a bigger home, his body started sending him mixed signals. His face became red and he experienced fatigue, but he concluded he'd overworked and perhaps stirred up allergies when he pulled out some old juniper bushes. Within half a year he noticed muscular soreness as if he'd jogged several miles—when he hadn't. Weakness set in. One day he had difficulty walking up a flight of stairs.

Doctors were baffled by his symptoms. More than $50,000 worth of tests, innumerable blood samples, and muscle biopsies followed without resulting in any specific diagnosis. Some thought it was a rare condition called dermatomyositis, an inflammation of the muscles related to arthritic conditions, but it didn't fit all the clinical criteria. Harlan and Linda were increasingly frustrated by the lack of information and, with it, the lack of hope that he could get better. In six weeks, his condition deteriorated so rapidly that he concluded he would die soon. He made sure his will was up to date and wrote letters to his five children, to be opened after his death.

Things got worse. Complications from testing caused his appendix to flare up, requiring an emergency appendectomy the day of their wedding anniversary. Shortly afterward, Harlan developed shingles. He and Linda—and their praying, fasting congregation—wondered if it could get any worse. It did. He next developed trigeminal neuralgia, a spontaneous, excruciating pain involving the branches of the fifth cranial nerve. Medical journals describe this as one of the most painful afflictions known to mankind. At its worst, Harlan would be crippled by facial pain five to six times a day, each episode lasting up to eight minutes.

"There was nothing I could do but lay on the floor and scream at the top of my lungs," he says. "The pain was so horrible I cannot describe it. Nobody could do anything for it, either. My children would come to my side during these episodes and pray, pat my back, bring me a wet towel, and encourage me to remember it would pass. That's all they could do."

God Knows How Much We Can Handle

Harlan says that these months of unbearable pain and uncertainty were what classic spiritual writers call "the dark night of the soul."

"Many times I felt God was not listening to my prayers," he says. "I was so sick, I couldn't even hold my Bible to read it. I had to rely on Scripture I'd memorized."

He especially grieved for his children—the possibility of not living to see them grow up and the picture they were getting of a God who wouldn't answer their fervent prayers for Daddy to get well.

"We didn't have any answers for the children," Linda says. "I couldn't lie to them and tell them that Daddy would get better, because we honestly didn't know what the future held."

The terrified Hebrews didn't know what their future held, either. They told Moses, "We sinned when we spoke against the Lord and against you. Pray that the Lord will take the snakes away from us" (Num. 21:7). When Moses prayed, God told him to hammer out a bronze snake and attach it to a pole. Anyone who was bitten could be healed simply by looking at the bronze snake.

Several things are significant here. First, notice that they explicitly confessed their sin. They knew they'd wronged both God and Moses when they complained about God's provision. They knew only God's power could remove the plague of snakes—they'd learned that lesson back in Egypt! Second, they had to accept an answer from God that wasn't what they expected. They wanted the snakes removed. God left the vipers around but provided the means for healing.

That's how God sometimes works. We ask him to take away an illness or a difficult situation. But he leaves us in it, providing another way to show his power. Paul took note of that important principle when he recounted this point of history in his letter to the Corinthians. "We should not test the Lord," he wrote, "as some of them did—and were killed by snakes. And do not grumble, as some of them did—and were killed by the destroying angel" (1 Cor. 10:9-10). Then he adds:

> No temptation has seized you except what is common to man. And God is faithful; he will not let you be tempted beyond what you can bear. But when you are tempted, he will also provide a way out so that you can stand up under it. (1 Corinthians 10:13)

The Greek word translated "temptation" here is broader than a compulsion to sin. It embraces tests and trials that can, in God's permissive wisdom, bring benefit in our spiritual growth. The passage provides two marvelous promises. First, we won't be given anything harder than we can bear. And second, God will be right there helping us when we think we can't stand it any longer. Job, the Old Testament saint who suffered greatly, expressed it another way when he affirmed that God cared about his pain: "Even now my witness is in heaven; my advocate is on high" (Job 16:19).

When Harlan wasn't healed, his family experienced both those promises through their church family. "We saw Christ in how people ministered to us," Linda says. "They just overwhelmed us with love and concern."

Two men came to Harlan and told him that they would help raise his children if Harlan died. They'd help Linda in whatever way they could and make sure the three boys got to ball games and were included in other male activities. Hundreds of cards and letters poured into their mailbox. Many shared Scriptures that had helped when they had suffered, providing Harlan with snatches of God's Word when he was too weak to lift his own Bible. One woman paid to have her housekeeper clean the Humistons' home for two months. People regularly took the Humiston children to their homes for a day or an overnight stay, especially alert to childcare needs during Harlan's medical appointments. Men helped with yard work and took care of Harlan's vehicles—all without being asked. At Christmas, a layman who moonlighted as Santa Claus at a local shopping center made a special visit to the children. Others hung up the outdoor lights and took the family to cut a Christmas tree.

For several months, meals were delivered to their door, often with a card of encouragement. "We received each meal as coming from the hand of Jesus," Harlan says. "Every meal was just great. It became obvious to us that this was the very body of Christ, manifesting itself to us through the church."

Up with Jesus, Down with Grumbling

God's bronze snake to cure Snakesville was a highly unlikely solution. Why make a pretend snake to banish the power of the real ones? In fact, making the image of a snake went against everything the people had been taught about worshiping God. Earlier they'd been told not to make images that could be used for worship (Ex. 20:4-6). They were aware of the animals or half-human/half-animal figures worshiped by pagan cultures like their former Egyptian neighbors. Historically, a snake was used as a fertility symbol in the temple of the Jebusites in Jerusalem. Bronze serpent images have also been found in other parts of Palestine. In addition, for the Hebrews, snakes or serpents represented a negative idea; most cultures and people despised or feared snakes. And it was a snake that was associated with Satan tempting Eve in the Garden of Eden (Gen. 3:1-15).

God's command to make a bronze snake sounded like a detestable instruction. But he was transforming something hated into something good, for when the Israelites looked at this powerless piece of brass, God's power intervened and healed them of their snake wounds.

Unfortunately, this old snake became a sacred cow. Hundreds of years later, when Hezekiah cleaned out the neglected temple, workmen found the old bronze snake still rattling around. The people called it "Nehushtan" (which sounds like the Hebrew for "bronze," "snake," and "unclean thing") and burned incense to it (2 Kings 18:4). Hezekiah broke it into pieces and sent it out on the garbage cart.

But God wasn't finished with that bronze snake. Hundreds of years later, during his conversation with Nicodemus, Jesus himself referred to the ancient symbol to help Nicodemus understand his point: "Just as Moses lifted up the snake in the desert, so the Son of Man must be lifted up, that everyone who believes in him may have eternal life" (John 3:14-15). Jesus would be lifted up on a cross on a high hill near Jerusalem. He would die in place of all who deserved to die spiritually forever because their sin-debt separated them from a holy God. His death would cancel that debt, but only if a person believed that Jesus indeed was dying on his or her behalf. The Israelites who looked to the bronze snake could attain extended physical life. Those who looked to Christ on the cross could attain eternal life.

I find it intriguing that the medical community uses as its symbol the caduceus, a winged staff with two serpents twined around it. You see it on medical emblems, stationery, ambulances, even the bracelets people wear to provide emergency medical information. While the caduceus is drawn from Greek mythology, I find it interesting that it is so similar to the serpent on the staff that Moses raised up for the healing of God's people. Despite the secular trappings of medicine, ultimately healing comes from Christ at Calvary. This does not mean that he removes every disease that attacks our bodies. Sometimes he heals miraculously; sometimes he heals through medical assistance. Other times, he allows pain to reside in our lives to teach us more about him and his sufficiency.

The apostle Paul grasped this when he finally came to terms with his "thorn in the flesh" (2 Cor. 12:7). Whatever Paul's affliction was, it was a tormenting condition he called a "messenger of Satan." He never blamed God for making him suffer; he only accepted that God allowed this condition. And Paul, through whom God had healed others so many times, had to accept that God was answering no to his own request for healing. Instead, God said he would give Paul an abundant supply of supernatural grace to live with his condition: "My grace is sufficient for you, for my power is made perfect in weakness" (2 Cor. 12:9).

We Are Weak, but He Is Strong

There's a gospel chorus with the line, "Let the weak say I am strong." To non-Christians, that just doesn't make sense. Our culture tells us that you get strong and then stronger. God's way is different. The greater our weakness, the greater our strength when we look to Jesus, for he fills the gaps of our feebleness with his power. That's why Paul could affirm the contradiction, "When I am weak, then I am strong" (2 Cor.

12:10). When his life was filled with insults, hardship, persecution, and difficulty, then he knew that Christ had more room to work.

From his classroom of pain, Harlan experienced that same truth. Doctors still couldn't get to the bottom of his sickness, though eventually his pain attacks faded. Physical therapy, the encouragement he gleaned from Norman Cousins' book *The Biology of Hope*, and especially the prayers and concern of his congregation and family started Harlan back up the ladder to health. Less than two years after his first symptoms—and while still in the process of recovery—he resumed full-time pastoral duties. He learned to pace himself. He grew a beard to protect his flushed, sun-sensitive face. And God added a new joy: the birth of a sixth child, a son.

As Harlan continues to live with this undiagnosed condition, he admits he's a changed man. He expressed some of those changes in his first sermons about six months after the worst of his illness. Still so weak he needed to sit on a stool by the pulpit, he told how his family saw Christ in the flood of caring they received. He also gained a perspective on grumbling.

Linda says she's still processing the implications of Harlan's two years of illness. But one thing she learned was that she didn't have to be afraid. "At first I feared being left a widow with five children and losing somebody I loved very much," she says. "I feared not knowing what was going to happen or when it was going to happen." Then this thought kept playing in her mind: Fear is not from God. Several verses affirmed that, including "God hath not given us the spirit of fear" (2 Tim. 1:7; KJV).

When Harlan's excruciating pain attacks abated, Linda was grateful for the little things they often had taken for granted. "It was wonderful to be able to go out to a restaurant together and not worry if he'd have a pain attack," she says, "or even just to get a full night's sleep. These things were taken away while Harlan was ill, but now they are given back. They are special gifts."

The couple also learned, from the days in hospitals and clinics, that whatever suffering they endure, someone else is going through worse. "We're grateful for what we have," Linda says. "We can't complain."

During the early part of Harlan's illness, Linda shared with him how God showed her they were like sheep being sheared by God. "God was telling us, don't fight, don't kick, or you will get nicked," she says. "We were to lay very still while this was happening."

"That helped," says Harlan, "because I tend to fight back if my family is attacked. So I quit fighting. I decided that if we had to go through this, we would. We'd be still before the Lord." A few months later, Linda felt impressed that the "shearing" was done, and they should fight for Harlan's health.

"I can't say my illness was a spiritual high point," says Harlan. "For six months, I didn't 'do it well.' I was fearful and worried and all the things a Christian should not be. But now that I'm past the crisis, I don't believe it showed me to be spiritually immature. Instead, it was a sign of the seriousness of what I went through. God gave me grace and told me he loved me. Being so sick changed my life. It deepened my ability to minister."

The writer of Hebrews talks of looking to Jesus, the author and perfecter of our faith, who endured the cross. At bottom, that's where grumbling settles out. We can express our anger at God for our pain—or we can move through that anger and be reconciled to him, trusting him for what we cannot understand.

When we leave our complaints at the foot of the cross—in the dirt stained with his blood—we are changed forever. When that happens, we'll find ourselves within sight of our own Promised Land. The next chapter puts us on the banks for that crossing.

Mileposts

1. What are some things you think you can legitimately

complain about? Write them down. Then read Job 1:21-22 and decide what God thinks of your list.

2. Among Jesus' cries from the cross was this: "My God, my God, why have you forsaken me?" (Matt. 27:46). Why do you think Jesus felt forsaken? Would you ever have the same reasons when you feel far from God? Consider Colossians 1:19-20 and 2 Corinthians 5:21 for how the cross eliminates our separation from God.

3. One source of grumbling is pride; that is, we think we deserve better than we get. What perspective do you get from Ecclesiastes 7:8?

4. A complainer is one who speaks first and thinks later. What help could you derive from Psalm 141:3-4?

5. Some verses are strong words to hang onto when you go through trials that seem to have no solution and God seems far away. Put this one in your soul: "My grace is sufficient for you, for my power is made perfect in weakness" (2 Cor. 12:9).

Take possession of the land and settle in it, for I have given
you the land to possess.—Numbers 33:53

13
From Whiners to Winners

Disbelief and Appropriation

Sooner or later, all family roads lead to a theme park. It happened for us the spring Inga turned five. She and brother Zach, six and a half, had been exposed to enough of one park's hoopla to almost taste it. Knowing how children can't wait, we decided to keep our spring break vacation extravaganza a secret until Inga's March 27 birthday.

While their dad went down to the travel agent and committed a chunk of his teacher's salary to tickets and transportation, I clandestinely sewed some roller-coaster print fabric into a birthday jumpsuit for Inga. (Jumpsuits better suit this perpetual-motion machine who began swan-diving out of her crib at eighteen months. I'm sure she's related to bouncy Tigger of Winnie the Pooh fame!)

On birthday night she was enthroned on the sofa, in ecstasy over every gift she opened. We kept the package with her jumpsuit for the last, because with it we'd make the announcement of our spring break plans.

Her eyes danced as she saw the print. And when her dad announced she'd wear it to the theme park, she couldn't believe it.

"For real?" she gasped in a higher-than-usual shriek as she

went bounce-bounce-bounce on the couch. "I've wanted to go there ALL MY LIFE!" Bounce, bounce, bounce some more.

I could hardly settle her down to sleep that night. She was close to tears with excitement over finally going on her dream vacation.

I suspect she takes after her mom in the emotions department. Whenever I drag out my wedding album, the children hoot over the picture of Dad and Mom coming down the aisle after the ceremony. Dad's beaming, having finally, at age thirty-six, conquered the rituals involved in claiming a wife. Mom is red-nosed and squinting, trying her best to hold back tears from her own thirty-four years of waiting. "Did you really cry, Mom?" the kids ask. Yes, I did. The heirloom handkerchief I clutched along with a bouquet got a good workout.

I've known the tears of sorrow and disappointment—broken relationships, the deaths of my parents, difficult job situations. But I've also known the times of joy when tears say what our emotions cannot: a wedding day, the birth of a healthy child, a graduation, an overwhelming honor. Such things chill and thrill us to our toes. Many of them we anticipate for a long time—like Inga's trip to her funland. We've endured hardship and sacrifice on their behalf. And when they come—oh, the unexplainable, unbelievable joy.

Here at Last!

I sometimes wonder what emotions marked the day the Israelites entered their Promised Land. I envision the priests as the muddy floodwaters of the Jordan grabbed their ankles, and they struggled to hold the shrouded Ark of the Covenant, their hearts beating hard with anticipation of what God would do.

It had been a long, hard forty years to this point. Egypt was a faint memory, because those who would enter Canaan had either been children in Egypt or had been born during the four decades of wandering. The bones of their parents and grandparents lay in sandy graves all over the desert, in accordance with God's judgment on that generation for faithlessness at Kadesh Barnea. They lived as nomads for nearly forty years, never knowing a home, never settling and cultivating crops, living off a miraculous though monotonous food called manna. From day to day they never knew if the cloud of God's presence would allow them to stay or command them to move again. You can sense the despair of rootlessness in Numbers 33, the itinerary of the wanderings. "They left," "they camped"—over and over those two phrases describe the sites whose names would defeat a spelling bee champ and whose markers have faded with time.

I can imagine my children's reactions if I'd told them we wouldn't get to their big-time playgound for forty years. "First, we'll go to the county park at Monitor and sleep in the car for a week," I'd say. "Then we'll roll on over to Cashmere and set up house in the car again. After that, maybe we'll camp on some side road in Peshastin, Dryden, and Leavenworth"—all towns within thirty miles. No way! My children wanted to get to that park as fast as they could.

But it was not so for the Israelites. They wandered—and they wondered. And as we read the place names where they camped, we remember some of the lessons they learned. These are lessons for us, too, for they mark our progress in spiritual growth.

Those lessons begin even before the Numbers summary, with the story of slavery and its call for *hope amidst despair*. Next, there's the lesson of *duty*, targeted at those who feel unworthy of God's call. Then Numbers 33 picks up the rest:

The lesson of fortitude. "They left Pi Hahiroth and passed through the sea into the desert" (Num. 33:8). Emancipated after a series of terrifying, God-ordained plagues, they faced a bridgeless body of water. God spread apart the waters like a curtain and sent them across the sea despite their fears that the wall of water might collapse and drown them. Fortitude shod their feet on that impossible road.

When we cry, "I can't make it!" God says, "Sure you can.

Just get going. I'm right beside you." It's easier for us to talk about something than actually do it. When I was a little girl, in the days when world travel was the privilege of the wealthy, my father loved to go to travelogue slide shows. For a couple of dollars' admission, he could travel vicariously to Japan, Greece, or Russia via the slides and commentary. But it wasn't quite the same as getting on a boat or plane and actually going to those sites. God wants us to apply for our travel papers and get going to the destination he has in mind. He wants us to claim the courage to leave our comfort zones.

The lesson of forgiveness. "When they had traveled for three days in the Desert of Etham, they camped at Marah. They left Marah and went to Elim, where there were twelve springs and seventy palm trees" (vv. 8-9). They had so much to be thankful for: their lives, freedom, the guidance of God in a blazing cloud above them. But thirst raged in their throats. The first water source, Marah, was bitter until Moses obeyed God and tossed in a stick to make it palatable. Then God led them to another, more abundant source of water.

Bitterness to sweetness, anger to forgiveness. For us, Marah pictures the cross of Christ, able to turn any foulness into something good. When the "root of bitterness" invades our lives, we need to let Christ deal with the contaminants in our spirits. Only then can he lead us to another place where we can know the sweet refreshing peace of his presence.

The lesson of thankfulness. "They left the Red Sea and camped in the Desert of Sin" (v. 11). After all God had done, they still grumbled. Manna wasn't gourmet fare—or even the melons, leeks, and cucumbers they savored in Egypt. Their appetites weren't ready for the "bread of angels" (Psalm 78:25). What God provided, they rejected.

Suppose when I gave Inga her roller-coaster print jumpsuit, she'd turned up her nose and said, "Ugh, I'd rather wear my baby clothes!" Not only would they not fit, I'd already given them away! She couldn't go back to size eighteen months any more than the Hebrews could eat like

Egyptians again. As God's chosen people, they also had a chosen diet.

God has chosen a diet for us, too. Our manna is his Word and promises. We can choose to complain about what comes our way, or feast on his Word and find it satisfying.

The lesson of trust. "They left Alush and camped at Rephidim, where there was no water for the people to drink" (Num. 33:14). Again thirst came. Discouragement quickly followed. But God said, "You saw before that I am trustworthy. Trust me again." Crunch went Moses' staff on a rock, and out flowed a steady stream.

A friend's adult daughter has tried to quench her thirst for meaning in life in all the wrong places. Several have joined this friend in praying that someday her daughter will come to the Rock—to Jesus Christ—and find that he is all she needs. She can trust him with those needs for survival and love. She can trust him to give focus to her life.

The lesson of anticipation. "They left Rephidim" (v. 15) after battling the Amalekites. When these deceitful distant cousins seeped out of the hillsides and attacked Hebrew stragglers, the rest of the Hebrew nation feared defeat. But the Amalekites didn't have a hotline to heaven. As Aaron and Hur kept Moses' arms raised in intercession and inspiration, the battle turned.

Prayer works! When we think there are no options, when the enemy seems too strong, we easily forget that prayer knows no obstacles. Prayer can be hard work, but we cannot give up. God will be faithful to hear and answer our prayers.

The lesson of self-control. "[They] camped in the Desert of Sinai" (v. 15). There, at the foot of Mt. Sinai, they waited for the greatest piece of writing ever, authored by God himself. But waiting was hard. When Moses took too long, they lost their patience and backslid into idolatry. In this sad scene, everybody lost control. Aaron yielded to the people's whining. The people gave themselves over to idol worship. And Moses, in a fit of righteous anger, flung to the ground the precious stone tablets from God.

There are few people who don't have dark chapters in their lives, times when they lost patience and either flirted with or thoroughly indulged in sinful behavior. They couldn't wait for God's best, and they crashed. But the hope of this incident is found in God's mercy. He gave Moses a second copy of the Law, and he gave the Israelites a second chance. For us, he provides the Cross and the promise that "if anyone is in Christ, he is a new creation" (2 Cor. 5:17). God can pull us off the floor and help us start over.

The lesson of remembrance. "They . . . camped at Kibroth Hattaavah" (v. 16). Two things happened here: wildfires on the outskirts and a second helping of quail, which turned deadly. Both judgments could be traced to spiritual coolness. In the first judgment, fires came to the outer rim of the camp where people lived farthest from the worship area and its reminders of God. In the second, the rabble—foreigners who tagged along for the Exodus—stoked appetites for something other than what God was providing. Their whining for meat brought quail and a plague that left the bodies of many at Kibroth Hattaavah.

Neither event would have happened had the people simply remembered that the God who had miraculously brought them this far would finish the job. We get that same lesson when people we live with, work with, or socialize with challenge our determination to follow God even when times are tough. When we stake our futures on our history with God, we bring him glory.

The lesson of certainty. "They . . . camped at Kadesh, in the Desert of Zin" (v. 36). Poised on the back step to the Promised Land, the Israelites sent twelve spies to explore the territories. Two were optimists; ten were pessimists who encouraged the people to turn against Moses and God. They spread propaganda that it would be better to die in slavery in Egypt than face extermination by the large and powerful people already living in Canaan. It was a human conclusion, one that negated the possibility of God helping them take over Canaan just as he had helped them flee Egypt.

Eighteenth-century British writer Samuel Johnson once observed, "He is no wise man who will quit a certainty for an uncertainty." Perhaps there were unknowns in Canaan. But there was also one rock-bottom certainty: God had prepared this land for them and had promised to settle them in it. Whenever we're faced with major life changes, that truth should come back to us. Our promised land may have its giants and battles—relationship challenges, financial hardship, health crises—but God goes with us.

The lesson of submission. During their lengthy stay in the Desert of Sinai, two of the priestly tribes grumbled about God's blueprint for the priesthood. Pride caused them to defy God; judgment came swiftly. But the Hebrews didn't learn that lesson well enough, for later others attempted to remodel God's ordained system of worship. Again, swift judgment upheld God's holiness.

Today, we are surrounded by those who want to adjust the requirements of faith in Christ. They want to make Christian faith easier or more accommodating to their lifestyle. I have a friend who gravitated to a cult that claims to fit all religions, because she doesn't believe the Bible came from God. Others add to the gospel. God, however, simply calls us to submit to his Word. It may not be popular, but it's God's will.

The lesson of reconciliation. "They left Mount Hor and camped at Zalmonah" (v. 41). Despite a God-given victory over attacking Canaanites, grumbling again hit the Hebrew camp. Egypt began to look good to them again. So God punished them with a plague of snakes. The remedy: healing manifested by looking at a bronze snake on a pole. Confession resulted in reconciliation with God.

Sometimes it takes pain to bring us back to reconciliation with God. Sinful choices hurt us and those who love us. I think of the couple whose son dropped deeper and deeper into alcoholism and drug abuse before he bottomed out and came back to his parents—and to God. Pain can also cause us to see Christ's love in a new way, personalizing the agony he endured to make it possible for us to have a relationship with a holy God.

The lesson of appropriation. "There on the plains of Moab they camped along the Jordan" (v. 49). Was it really coming true? Was this the time for which they'd waited nearly half a century since leaving Egypt? Was this finally the time to fulfill the promise given Abraham five centuries earlier? God answered: "Take possession of the land and settle in it, for I have given you the land to possess" (Num. 33:53).

We know the rest of the story. Joshua, one of the two earlier optimistic spies and now Moses' successor, sent two spies to Jericho, gate-city to Canaan. The spies said, "Go for it." The priests carried the ark to the swollen Jordan River and stepped in. Immediately, the upstream waters ceased flowing, piling up at the town of Adam, about twenty miles upstream. While the people crossed over: "The priests who carried the ark of the covenant of the LORD stood firm on dry ground in the middle of the Jordan, while all Israel passed by until the whole nation had completed the crossing on dry ground" (Josh. 3:17). It's too easy to skip over that verse. Consider that the priests preceded the people, stepping by faith into the river. Then they stood in their midst as people passed respectfully around the symbol of God's presence. God precedes us, he remains in our midst, and he follows behind to ensure our safety.

Then notice one more task after everyone had crossed over. Joshua asked a representative from each tribe to take a rock from the riverbed near where the priests stood with the ark. These they brought to the west bank of the Jordan, where they were stacked as a memorial:

> In the future, when your children ask you, "What do these stones mean?" tell them that the flow of the Jordan was cut off before the ark of the covenant of the Lord. When it crossed the Jordan, the waters of the Jordan were cut off. These stones are to be a memorial to the people of Israel forever. (Joshua 4:6-7)

Once the stones came out of the river bottom, the priests and the ark came to Canaan. The Exodus was complete. They had come from the despair of Egypt to the hope of Canaan. From blood, toil, and tears—to milk and honey. From the turbulent lessons of spiritual adolescence to a fuller, steadier walk with God.

I wonder how many times Jericho's new residents walked back to the riverbank to meditate by the mound of memorial stones. Their hearts must have beat hard with awe as they remembered the day those stones came out of the middle of the river.

Connecting with the Past

Whenever our family travels, we try to stop at historical markers along the freeways. But we get a ho-hum reaction from the children as we get out to stretch our legs and read those signs. Sometimes there's a spark, something special to help them imagine why this place was so important. I remember when we visited the Whitman mission site near Walla Walla, Washington, where Marcus and Narcissa Whitman and twelve others died in a massacre in 1847. As the children and I moved quietly over the marked compound, I tried to share with them my feelings about that tragic day. I asked them to imagine being in the mission when it happened. But I suspect the tie to history still wasn't there for them. That sort of awe and appreciation must come with maturity.

The summer I turned thirty-three, as part of a graduate tour, I was able to visit Washington, D.C. I took my place in line behind school groups at the exhibit of historical documents. I heard "Hey, cool" and "Wow!" from children up ahead. But as I moved past the guarded display of the Declaration of Independence, I was struck wordless. My heart beat hard as I thought of how the passions behind that document changed my life before it even began. I connected with history.

We need to follow the example of the Israelites at the

Jordan and establish our own memorials. They probably won't be piles of rocks. But there are other ways to commemorate the times when God helped you on your own "rocky roads."

For Karen and John Clark, a newborn Santa outfit is carefully tucked away as a reminder of answered prayer. Karen remembers the Christmas of 1986 as she watched her three sisters' babies play during their family Christmas. Karen was happy for them, but there was a lingering sadness; she was childless after eight years of marriage and many tests and procedures for infertility.

After Christmas, her mother mailed her a package along with a note: "I felt the Lord wanted me to send you this." As Karen opened the package and pulled out a newborn Santa outfit, her heart sank with a renewed sense of failure. She knew her mother intended the gift as a promise to pray, but the prospect of conceiving a child seemed to diminish by the month, even as Karen and John continued consulting doctors.

On April 1, as John continued his discipline of reading through the Bible, he came to the story in 2 Kings 4 about Elisha and the Shunammite woman. He felt God impressing on him that the promise to the Shunammite woman—that within a year she'd hold a son in her arms—was God's promise for him and Karen. In the meantime, Karen received word that she was pregnant. On December 21, Mary Elizabeth Clark was born. And she went home on Christmas Day—dressed like Santa.

A Memorials Idea

In our family, the memorials are wedged in a glass-fronted knick-knack case. We started filling that case the summer our adult Sunday school class featured a video on memorials by Garry and Anne Marie Ezzo of Growing Kids God's Way. We involved the family in deciding what symbols to use for God's lessons and help in our lives. Like the Jordan stones, our case has become a reminder of God's sovereignty in our lives.

Our memorial box, which hangs above the piano, now has twenty-two memorial symbols. Hospital bracelets represent faith-testing surgeries. An antique cross necklace, a gift from a long-ago neighbor, reminds me of how this woman who had no children of her own embraced me and my sister as if we were her own grandchildren. A miniature telephone reminds us of the phone call that put Rich back in touch with me after eight years of silence—and eventually led to our marriage. A Lifesaver candy recalls the time Rich nearly drowned while tubing down the Yakima River. Miniature books represent the way God has given me a writing ministry. A rolled paper labeled "mortgage" reminds us of how God honored our efforts to live frugally and pay off our house mortgage. An award pin, given Rich midway through his education career, marks how God directed him into teaching and blessed his faithfulness. And there are empty slots, too—for God is not done with us yet.

Neither was God done with the Israelites after they crossed into Canaan. Gaining their Promised Land inheritance meant overcoming enemies and obstacles. But they had trained for this for forty years. God took a bunch of whiners and taught them how to be winners. What better advice than what he gave through Joshua: "Be strong and courageous. Do not be terrified; do not be discouraged, for the Lord your God will be with you wherever you go" (Josh. 1:9). "Don't fall back into your old attitudes," Joshua was saying. "Don't let fear or despair color your future. If God's going with you, it will be okay."

We live in the middle of Washington State. Seattle is a three-and-a-half-hour drive west, and Spokane is the same distance east. Whenever we head for one of those cities, we can count on some back-seat complaints about an hour into the journey. We stave off their grumbling by saying, "In just a little bit we'll get to the Science Center," or "Soon we'll be at Aunt Judi's and see her Siamese cat." As we hit the weather-ravaged roadways on the mountain passes, and the children are jostled uncomfortably, we remind them that this is the way we have to go to get to the other side. There is no such thing as a smooth ride all the way.

When Do We Get There?

Often in life the same questions come up. "Am I there yet?" "Have I arrived spiritually?" The answer is that we don't "arrive" spiritually until God calls us to heaven. And yes, the journey will get rough. But God is faithful. He is with us. As Psalm 139:5 says, "You hem me in—behind and before." God wants us to think about heaven, but he also wants us to see the present journey as his training program for heaven. Someone once said, "We can get so caught up in thinking about Glory that we forget we are God's glory now." We'll be successful travelers when we reveal God's character in our words and deeds. Mark the words of this old German hymn:

> Sing praise to God who reigns above,
> The God of all creation,
> The God of power, the God of love,
> The God of our salvation;
> With healing balm my soul he fills,
> And every faithless murmur stills:
> To God all praise and glory.

He heals us; he fills us. He stills those faithless murmurs. Because of that, we'll bear it. We'll do it. We'll make it. We'll be thankful. We'll wait. We'll hang on. We'll take courage. We'll accept the difficulties. And we'll appropriate what God has promised.

Mileposts

1. Throughout this book we've followed the Exodus story of God's chosen people and applied their lessons to us. What does Ephesians 1:11-12 say about our "specialness"?

2. Moses was not permitted to enter Canaan because of his own disobedience (Num. 20:6-13). But the book of Deuteronomy holds his last instructions to the people he'd led for four decades. The yearning of his heart is put in a nugget in Deuteronomy 8:1-5. How does the instruction "remember" of verse 2 fit with that of "forget" in Philippians 3:13-14?

3. Even this book could become a twelve-stone memorial monument for your life. Have any of the first twelve chapters on spiritual attitudes spoken to your heart? Have you asked God to help you change negative words and deeds into actions that reflect his character? If you have, mark the date of that decision beside the appropriate chapter in the table of contents.

4. Someone has said, "God is both the promise maker and the promise keeper." From Joshua 1 choose a verse that encourages you to trust and love God.

5. Here's a golden promise to memorize for the spiritual journeys we all make: "He who began a good work in you will carry it on to completion until the day of Christ Jesus" (Phil. 1:6).

Notes

1. "Parents in Jail; Boy Can't Live Alone," *Wenatchee World* 5 September 1995: 11.

2. Louis O. Caldwell, *You Can Face Suffering* (Grand Rapids, MI: Baker Book House, 1978) 12.

3. J. Oswald Chambers, *Promised Land Living* (Chicago: Moody Press, 1984) 19.

4. Jerry Bridges, *Transforming Grace* (Colorado Springs, CO: NavPress, 1991) 183.

5. Quote by Samuel Smiles, *The Dictionary of Similes*, ed. Frank Wilstach (New York: Bonanza Books, 1974) 203.

6. Stephen Pile, *The Incomplete Book of Failures* (New York: E. P. Dutton, 1979) 165-67.

7. Skip Gray, "The Way of the Cross," *Discipleship Journal* 31 (1985): 8.

8. Don Baker, *The Way of the Shepherd* (Portland, OR: Multnomah Press, 1987) 24-25.

9. George MacDonald, *The Boyhood of Ranald Bannerman,* ed. Dan Hamilton (Wheaton, IL: Victor Books, 1987) 113.

10. E. Stanley Jones, *The Unshakable Kingdom and the Unchangeable Person* (New York: Harper and Row, 1972) 102.

11. "Harper's Index," *Harper's* February 1997: 13.

12. LeRoy Eims, "Why Obey God?" *Discipleship Journal* 31 (1985): 40.

13. "Hiker Trapped 8 Days Loses Impatience," Associated Press story in *Wenatchee World* 18 October 1996: 11.

14. Roy Hession, *The Calvary Road* (Fort Washington, PA: Christian Literature Crusade, 1950) 48.

15. Quoted in *The Oxford Dictionary of Quotations*, 3rd. ed. (Oxford, Eng.: Oxford Univ. Pr., 1980) 126.

16. "Names in the News," *Wenatchee World* 23 July 1996: 17.